ISSUES THAT CONCERN YOU

Junk Food

Ronald D. Lankford, Jr., *Book Editor*

GREENHAVEN PRESS
A part of Gale, Cengage Learning

Detroit • New York • San Francisco • New Haven, Conn • Waterville, Maine • London

Christine Nasso, *Publisher*
Elizabeth Des Chenes, *Managing Editor*

© 2011 Greenhaven Press, a part of Gale, Cengage Learning

Gale and Greenhaven Press are registered trademarks used herein under license.

For more information, contact:
Greenhaven Press
27500 Drake Rd.
Farmington Hills, MI 48331-3535
Or you can visit our Internet site at gale.cengage.com

For product information and technology assistance, contact us at

Gale Customer Support, 1-800-877-4253
For permission to use material from this text or product, submit all requests online at www.cengage.com/permissions

Further permissions questions can be e-mailed to permissionrequest@cengage.com

Articles in Greenhaven Press anthologies are often edited for length to meet page require-ments. In addition, original titles of these works are changed to clearly present the main thesis and to explicitly indicate the author's opinion. Every effort is made to ensure that Greenhaven Press accurately reflects the original intent of the authors. Every effort has been made to trace the owners of copyrighted material.

Cover image copyright © Getty Images

LIBRARY OF CONGRESS CATALOGING-IN-PUBLICATION DATA

Junk food / Ronald D. Lankford, Jr., book editor.
   p. cm. -- (Issues that concern you)
 Includes bibliographical references and index.
 ISBN 978-0-7377-4954-0 (hardcover)
 1. Junk food--Health aspects. I. Lankford, Ronald D., 1962-
TX370.J862 2010
613.2--dc22

                                            2010019296

Printed in the United States of America
1 2 3 4 5 6 7 14 13 12 11 10

CONTENTS

Junk food and fast food have taken the center stage in countries like the United States and Britain as many experts have tied poor eating habits to obesity and multiple health problems. Described as food frequently high in fat, sugar, and salt content and providing little nutritional value, junk food has been blamed for high blood pressure, kidney stones, heart stress, and what a number of experts have called the obesity epidemic. As a result of this criticism, members of Congress and Parliament have considered taxing junk and fast food as a way to pay for increasing health care costs.

The impression that junk and fast food are a Western problem, however, is no longer accurate. Although junk food may not be available everywhere in the world, many developing countries have joined the United States and Britain in their love of fast and junk food. This change can be clearly seen in Romania, a country primarily devoid of McDonald's restaurants, soft drinks, and snack food before the collapse of its Communist government in 1989. Twenty years later Romania is experiencing the same crisis in relation to junk and fast food as many countries in the West.

Fast and Junk Food Arrive in Romania

In 1995 McDonald's opened its first restaurant in Romania and processed more than fifteen thousand transactions on its first day of business. Fifteen years later fifty McDonald's operate in the country. In 2002 Nestlé established a base of operations in Romania; in 2005 PepsiCo and General Mills bought out Romania's leading snack company, providing both companies with a factory to manufacture products for the entire country.

As the junk and fast food industries grew in Romania, a number of problems began to appear. At the beginning of 2010 it was estimated that more than half of Romania's 22 million people were overweight. The obesity rate had also doubled for ten-year-olds. Even as early as 2004 health experts in Romania had begun to worry about the impact of weight issues in relation to health. "If now we have a problem with diabetes we will have more problems, 2.5-fold problems in a few years if we [do] not [do] anything,"[1] obesity specialist Gabriela Roman told Radio Free Europe.

Government officials in Romania placed at least part of the blame for the rising obesity on the availability of junk food. Although a number of elements—such as lack of regular exercise—may also impact weight, Romanian officials believed that there was a clear connection between the growth of the fast and junk food industries in their country and the increase in overweight and obese citizens. "We can't just stand around doing nothing," Adrian Streinu-Cercel, secretary of state with the Health Ministry, explained at a press conference. "We have to re-educate Romanians on how to feed themselves properly."[2]

The Romanian Solution

A central part of that education will be focused on a junk food tax that the government plans to establish in 2010. By taxing junk food in much the same way that many countries tax cigarettes and alcohol, Romania's government hopes to accomplish two tasks. First, it plans to raise the overall price of junk food to help curb consumption, and second, it wants to use the money generated from the tax to fund health care. It is estimated that the tax could raise as much as $1.37 billion in new funds. The European Public Health Alliance supports the tax, noting, "Poor diet and lack of sufficient physical activity result in a situation whereby energy intake exceeds the amount being expended in our day to day lives. The increasing consumption of foods that are high in fats, salt and sugars . . . reflects and contributes to the worsening of this trend."[3]

A number of hurdles remain for the Romanian government, however. Which foods, for instance, will the government choose to tax? What criteria will be used to determine what is junk food

People in Bucharest, Romania, walk past a McDonald's. The Romanian government imposed a controversial tax on junk food in 2010.

and what is not? To accomplish these tasks, Romania's Health Ministry has studied the contents of forty thousand food and drink items. Other questions also remain, such as how high the tax will be and whether the tax, once instated, will actually curb junk food consumption.

As in other countries that have proposed a tax on junk food, the measure remains controversial. Critics charge that the government should focus on other issues, such as education. Critics have also accused the Romanian government of planning to exempt traditional foods such as kabobs that are also high in fat and to focus on Western junk food items. Finally, critics caution that adding a new tax at a time when Romania is experiencing a recession will be counterproductive.

Junk Food Is an International Issue

Romania's decision to tax junk food placed the nation in the media's spotlight at the beginning of 2010, but Romania was far from the only country experiencing problems in relation to junk food. A number of other countries, such as Taiwan, are also considering a junk food tax. In the United States, First Lady Michelle Obama has begun the Let's Move campaign to fight childhood obesity, and a number of countries—including Britain, Norway, and Sweden—have already banned junk food commercials on television during certain times of the day.

The issues of obesity and taxation are two of the many topics examined in this anthology. In articles taken from magazines, newspapers, Web sites, and blogs, writers address the competing views surrounding the debate on junk and fast food. The appendix titled "What You Should Know About Junk Food" provides information for young people who may experience the issue in their own lives. A second appendix, titled "What You Should Do About Junk Food," offers information for young people to better understand the role that junk food plays in their own lives. With all of these features, *Issues That Concern You: Junk Food* provides an excellent resource for anyone interested in this timely issue.

Notes

1. Quoted in Kathleen Knox, "Eastern Europe: Experts Chew Over Problem of Obesity," Radio Free Europe, May 9, 2004. www.rferl .org/content/article/1053036.html.

2. Quoted in Mihaela Rodina, "Row in Romania over Bid to Impose Major Junk Food Tax," Yahoo! February 11, 2010. http:// news.yahoo.com/s/afp/20100212/lf_afp/romaniahealthobesity tax_20100212063021.

3. European Public Health Alliance, "Open Letter," February 2, 2010. www.euractiv.com/sites/all/euractiv/files/Open_Letter_to_ Romanian_Government_FINAL.pdf.

ONE

The Food Industry Tries to Alter Perceptions of Junk Food

Adam Voiland

In this selection Adam Voiland has learned from two researchers the ten things that the junk food industry does not want the public to know. Voiland points out that junk food makers spend $1.6 billion per year to advertise to children, and that the same companies minimize health concerns related to the products they sell. Furthermore, he notes, although these companies claim to offer healthy alternatives, the alternatives are seldom healthier. Voiland explains that the junk food industry also spends a great deal of money to discredit individuals and institutions that are critical of the industry. Voiland is a science and medicine writer.

With America's obesity problem among kids reaching crisis proportions, even junk food makers have started to claim they want to steer children toward more healthful choices. In a study released earlier this year [2008], the Centers for Disease Control and Prevention reported that about 32 percent of children were overweight but not obese, 16 percent were obese, and

11 percent were extremely obese. Food giant PepsiCo, for example, points out on its website that "we can play an important role in helping kids lead healthier lives by offering healthy product choices in schools." The company highlights what it considers its healthier products within various food categories through a "Smart Spot" marketing campaign that features green symbols on packaging. PepsiCo's inclusive criteria . . . award spots to foods of dubious nutritional value such as Diet Pepsi, Cap'n Crunch cereal, reduced-fat Doritos, and Cheetos, as well as to more nutritious products such as Quaker Oatmeal and Tropicana Orange Juice.

But are wellness initiatives like Smart Spot just marketing ploys? Such moves by the food industry may seem to be a step in the right direction, but ultimately makers of popular junk foods have an obligation to stockholders to encourage kids to eat more—not less—of the foods that fuel their profits, says David Ludwig, a pediatrician and the co-author of a commentary published in this week's [October 18, 2008] *Journal of the American Medical Association [JAMA]* that raises questions about whether big food companies can be trusted to help combat obesity. Ludwig and article co-author Marion Nestle, a professor of nutrition at New York University, both of whom have long histories of tracking the food industry, spoke with *U.S. News* and highlighted 10 things that junk food makers don't want you to know about their products and how they promote them.

1. Junk food makers spend billions advertising unhealthy foods to kids. According to the Federal Trade Commission, food makers spend some $1.6 billion annually to reach children through the traditional media as well as the Internet, in-store advertising, and sweepstakes. An article published in 2006 in the *Journal of Public Health Policy* puts the number as high as $10 billion annually. Promotions often use cartoon characters or free giveaways to entice kids into the junk food fold. PepsiCo has pledged that it will advertise only "Smart Spot" products to children under 12.

2. The studies that food producers support tend to minimize health concerns associated with their products. In fact, according to a review led by Ludwig of hundreds of studies that looked at the health effects of milk, juice, and soda, the likelihood of conclu-

"That's $7.99, 2,400 calories and 125 grams of fat," cartoon by Dan Rosandich. www.Cartoon Stock.com.

sions favorable to the industry was several times higher among industry-sponsored research than studies that received no industry funding. "If a study is funded by the industry, it may be closer to advertising than science," he says.

3. *Junk food makers donate large sums of money to professional nutrition associations.* The American Dietetic Association [ADA], for example, accepts money from companies such as Coca-Cola, which get access to decision makers in the food and nutrition marketplace via ADA events and programs. As Nestle notes in her blog and discusses at length in her book *Food Politics*, the group even distributes nutritional fact sheets that are directly sponsored by specific industry groups. [One fact sheet], for example, which is sponsored by an industry group that promotes lamb, rather unsurprisingly touts the nutritional benefits of lamb. The ADA's reasoning: "These collaborations take place with the understanding that ADA does not support any program or message that does not correspond with ADA's science-based healthful-eating messages and positions," according to the group's president, dietitian Martin

Yadrick. "In fact, we think it's important for us to be at the same table with food companies because of the positive influence that we can have on them."

4. *More processing means more profits, but typically makes the food less healthy.* Minimally processed foods such as fresh fruits and vegetables obviously aren't where food companies look for profits. The big bucks stem from turning government-subsidized commodity crops—mainly corn, wheat, and soybeans—into fast foods, snack foods, and beverages. High-profit products derived from these commodity crops are generally high in calories and low in nutritional value.

5. *Less-processed foods are generally more satiating than their highly processed counterparts.* Fresh apples have an abundance of fiber and nutrients that are lost when they are processed into applesauce. And the added sugar or other sweeteners increase the number of calories without necessarily making the applesauce any more filling. Apple juice, which is even more processed, has had almost all of the fiber and nutrients stripped out. This same stripping out of nutrients, says Ludwig, happens with highly refined white bread compared with stone-ground whole wheat bread.

6. *Many supposedly healthy replacement foods are hardly healthier than the foods they replace.* In 2006, for example, major beverage makers agreed to remove sugary sodas from school vending machines. But the industry mounted an intense lobbying effort that persuaded lawmakers to allow sports drinks and vitamin waters that—despite their slightly healthier reputations—still can be packed with sugar and calories.

7. *A health claim on the label doesn't necessarily make a food healthy.* Health claims such as "zero trans fats" or "contains whole wheat" may create the false impression that a product is healthy when it's not. While the claims may be true, a product is not going to benefit your kid's health if it's also loaded with salt and sugar or saturated fat, say, and lacks fiber or other nutrients. "These claims are calorie distracters," adds Nestle. "They make people forget about the calories." Dave DeCecco, a spokesperson for PepsiCo, counters that the intent of a labeling program such as Smart Spot is simply to help consumers pick a healthier choice

Critics say that products produced by PepsiCo, such as those above, include labeling information implying that they have nutritional benefits when, in fact, they are often loaded with fats and sugars.

within a category. "We're not trying to tell people that a bag of Doritos is healthier than asparagus. But, if you're buying chips, and you're busy, and you don't have a lot of time to read every part of the label, it's an easy way to make a smarter choice," he says.

8. *Food industry pressure has made nutritional guidelines confusing.* As Nestle explained in *Food Politics*, the food industry has a history of preferring scientific jargon to straight talk. As far back as 1977, public health officials attempted to include the advice "reduce consumption of meat" in an important report called *Dietary Goals for the United States*. The report's authors capitulated to intense pushback from the cattle industry and used this less-direct and more ambiguous advice: "Choose meats, poultry, and fish which will reduce saturated fat intake." Overall, says

Nestle, the government has a hard time suggesting that people eat less of anything.

9. *The food industry funds front groups that fight antiobesity public health initiatives.* Unless you follow politics closely, you wouldn't necessarily realize that a group with a name like the Center for Consumer Freedom (CCF) has anything to do with the food industry. In fact, Ludwig and Nestle point out, this group lobbies aggressively against obesity-related public health campaigns—such as the one directed at removing junk food from schools—and is funded, according to the Center for Media and Democracy, primarily through donations from big food companies such as Coca-Cola, Cargill, Tyson Foods, and Wendy's.

10. *The food industry works aggressively to discredit its critics.* According to the new *JAMA* article, the Center for Consumer Freedom boasts that "[our strategy] is to shoot the messenger. We've got to attack [activists'] credibility as spokespersons." . . .

The bottom line, says Nestle, is quite simple: Kids need to eat less, include more fruits and vegetables, and limit the junk food.

TWO

There Is No Such Thing as Junk Food

Stanley Feldman

> Stanley Feldman is a medical doctor and the author of a
> series of textbooks on anesthesia. In this selection Feldman
> argues that there is no such thing as junk food: Anything
> that qualifies as "food" cannot be "junk." Although ham-
> burgers, he notes, may be vilified as junk food, they are
> healthier than some nonjunk food items. Part of the preju-
> dice against hamburgers and potato chips, Feldman notes,
> is rooted in snobbery, but a great deal of "fashionable"
> food is no more healthy than so-called junk food. The
> problem, Feldman concludes, is not with food but with
> eaters; too many people overeat, becoming "junk eaters."

THE MYTH: Junk food causes ill health.
*THE FACT: There is no such thing as food that is bad and
food that is good for you.*

The term 'junk food' is an oxymoron. Either something is a
food, in which case it is not junk, or it has no nutritional value,
in which case it cannot be called a food. It cannot be both. Ask
most people what they understand by the term and they think
of McDonald's hamburgers. None of their explanations for why
hamburgers are junk food makes any sense; rather, they believe
hamburgers are the cause of serious health problems because they

Stanley Feldman, *Panic Nation: Exposing the Lies We're Told About Health and Food*. London: John
Blake Publishing, 2005. © Text copyright Stanley Feldman and Vincent Marks. Reproduced
by permission.

have been told it is so. Any food eaten to excess is, as [Swiss physician] Paracelsus said in 1538, potentially harmful. Morgan Spurlock ate a diet composed solely of McDonald's food for a month for his film *Super Size Me*. At the end of that time, he felt unwell and had put on weight. Had he eaten a similar weight of 'healthy' sardines for the same time he would no doubt have felt just as unwell and put on just as much weight! No particular individual component of any mixed diet is harmful. The concept of 'good foods' and 'junk foods' is nonsense.

Some rather ill-informed individuals have so convinced themselves of the dangers of hamburgers that they have suggested taxing them or giving them a red warning label. . . . Why hamburgers should be considered such a threat to our health that they should be singled out for taxation defies reason. Why should mincing a piece of beef turn it from being a 'good food' into one that is such dangerous 'junk' that it needs to be taxed in order to dissuade people from eating it? What would happen if, instead of mincing the meat, it was chopped into chunks and made into boeuf bourguignon [a beef stew]—should it be taxed at only 50 per cent? To try to justify this illogical proposal, these self-appointed food experts tell us that hamburgers contain more fat than a fillet steak. They fail to point out that the ratio of protein to fat in a hamburger is usually higher than in most lamb chops, and that most hamburgers contain less fat than a Sainsbury's Waldorf salad.

But, that aside, why should the fat be bad? Would these same people like to tax the cheese offered at the end of the meal because, after all, it contains the same basic animal fat as the hamburger? Or perhaps it is the hamburger bun that they feel is unhealthy. But the same self-appointed dietary experts would not object to a helping of food in the form of pasta or a slice or two of wholemeal brown bread (which, by the way, is the bread with the highest level of pesticide). The pasta, the bread and the bun produce a similar carbohydrate load in our food and are absorbed into the bloodstream as the same constituents. As for the tomato ketchup on the hamburger, it is rich in vitamin C and the antioxidant polyphenols that are supposed to keep cell degeneration and cancer at bay.

Food Is Food

There is no such thing as junk food. All food is composed of carbohydrate, fat and protein. An intake of a certain amount of each is essential for a healthy life. In addition, a supply of certain minerals, such as iron, calcium and tiny amounts of selenium, and a supply of vitamins, fibre, salt and fluid contribute to health. Once the necessary amounts of carbohydrate, fat and protein have been taken, any long-term surplus is stored as glycogen or fat in the body. Protein is protein whether it comes from an Aberdeen Angus steak or a McDonald's hamburger. It is broken up in the gut into its amino-acid building blocks, which are identical in both the hamburger and the steak; and although the

In his 2004 documentary film Super Size Me, *Michael Spurlock (pictured) ate only McDonald's food for a month, which, he says, left him overweight and feeling unwell. Author Stanley Feldman argues that the same results would occur from eating massive amounts of any food.*

relative amounts of each particular amino acid may vary slightly, this has no nutritional significance. These broken-down products of protein are absorbed into the bloodstream to be restructured into body proteins in the various cells of the body. Any excess ends up as fat. One source of animal protein is not necessarily of better value to the body than another, nor is it more or less fattening. A diet consisting only of Aberdeen Angus steak would be as 'junky' as one composed only of hamburgers. Similarly, animal fat is broken down and absorbed in the same way whether it originated in a hamburger, a lamb chop or the cheese on top of a pasta dish.

We need some fat in our diet, not only because it contains essential fat-soluble vitamins but also because it contributes much of the taste to foods. Very lean meat is tasteless unless enriched by a sauce containing fatty flavouring. No one would suggest that eating hamburgers and chips every day would constitute a good diet, but it would be better than one made up of Waldorf salad. The answer lies in a diet that is both varied and balanced.

The idea has grown up that some foods make you fat and others are slimming. It is true that pound for pound the fat in cheese contains about twice the calories of carbohydrate or protein but one eats much more carbohydrate and probably more protein than fat each day. It is the amount you eat that makes you fat.

Snobbery and Junk Food

One thing that the fast food industry has changed is the cost of food. Some would argue that it is now so readily available and cheap that it is not sufficiently rationed by price. As a result, people eat too much. In a world where some people are starving, this seems to be a perverse reason for objecting to the contribution made by the food industry. Many people of my generation can remember chicken being so expensive it was considered a luxury reserved for high days and holydays. It does suggest that the real cause of the problem of obesity is not the food or the ready availability of certain foods, it is a social phenomenon associated with affluence and the leisure time to enjoy eating. In other words, the

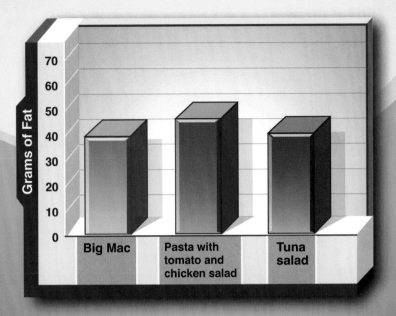

Taken from: British Broadcasting Corporation. www.bbc.co.uk.

'junk' appellation [label] should not be applied to the hamburger but to its consumer and his lifestyle.

We have been so indoctrinated about the evils of junk food, a concept so closely tied up with hamburgers that, if you were to ask the man in the street which was the better meal, lobster mayonnaise salad or a hamburger, he would almost certainly condemn the hamburger. In terms of its contribution to the food requirements of the body, the lobster mayonnaise, with its high cholesterol and fat and low-value protein, approaches the junk-food profile while a hamburger with tomato ketchup is much better value as a mixed food. A tomato, basil and chicken salad from Safeway is presented as 'healthy food' although it contains roughly the same amount of fat and calories as a Big Mac and chips (*Sunday Times*, August 2004). If, instead of eating a Big Mac, people were suddenly to start eating these salads, it is unlikely they would be any healthier or lose any weight.

There is no doubt that snobbery and cost contributes to the perception of what is called 'junk'. The term is associated with foods originating in the fast-food chains of America rather than those coming from 'foody' France, home of the *croque monsieur* [grilled ham and cheese] and foie gras [goose liver]; from Belgium, the country of *moules et frites* [mussels and french fries]; or from Italy with its creamy pastas covered with cheese. For a century, generations of Britons ate fried fish and chips, liberally dosed with salt and vinegar, without becoming dangerously overweight. However, when the fish protein is replaced by the meat of a hamburger or by Kentucky Fried Chicken, it suddenly becomes a national disaster.

Overeating and Junk Food

The present obsession with obesity has resulted in any food providing a high calorie content being labelled as 'junk'. It is obvious nonsense: cheese is good food, as are fish and chips and hamburgers. It is not the particular food that makes people fat, it is the amount of it that they eat. The three heaviest mammals—the whale, the elephant and the hippopotamus—are all vegetarians; they don't eat hamburgers, chips or crisps but they get fat. The whale is hugely fat—it is covered in fatty blubber—but most whales eat only plankton (which would no doubt qualify for the five-a-day portions of vegetables and fruit we are told we must eat). It is fat because it eats lots of plankton, it grazes continuously, it's the whale's lifestyle. It is not fat because it eats food containing a lot of calories. A person who also continuously nibbled food all day long would become fat even if he grazed on fruit and vegetables. A person who sits in front of the television eating bags of peanuts (a good food) is more likely to become fat than one eating the occasional hamburger.

There is often confusion between so-called junk food and fast food. A pizza can provide an excellent meal even if it is likely to be a little heavy on fats, whereas a cherry tart that took hours to make is likely to contain more carbohydrate—even before the cream has been added to increase its fat content. Neither is junk, and both contribute food essential for the nourishment of the body.

So what is junk? I suppose the nearest one comes to a substance that is not nourishing is water. Nevertheless, a fluid intake of about two litres a day (some of it as water) is essential for survival. Without salt we would all die. We need fat, protein and carbohydrate. Even fibre, which contributes so little towards our essential nutritional requirements that it could be considered a 'junk food', has a part to play in digestion. The lettuce and cucumber salad we are told we must eat every day to prevent us dying prematurely is made up of over 98 per cent water, while most of the rest is fibre and contributes little of nutritional value. We all know of children who have refused any salad or green vegetables and have grown up to be long-lived, healthy adults. Lettuce and cucumber would qualify for junk-food status but for the small amounts of water-soluble vitamins and antioxidants that they contain. Celery is said to require more energy in the eating than one gains from its consumption—that might qualify it for the label 'junk', but there is no evidence to suggest that it is in any way harmful.

Processed Foods

Since the junk food title makes no sense the food zealots have lined up another culprit in their search for something to ban, it is 'processed food'. Why processed food should be bad is not clear as it is difficult to find out exactly what they are. Since we eat relatively few foods without cleaning them, cooking them and flavouring them, it is difficult to see what particular processes are considered to be a health hazard. Those foods that are partially prepared in some way by the food industry are no different from those prepared at home although their culinary treatment is probably better controlled. The food we eat in restaurants is certainly processed but is it therefore bad? Do the food police seriously believe in some sinister plot by the food industry to introduce dangerous or harmful substances into the meals during the preparation process? Most evidence points to the meals prepared and served at home as being more likely to cause a health problem, such as food poisoning or obesity.

Certainly, some classical methods of preparation for preservation, such as pickling and salting of meat and the preparation of some bacon, introduces nitrates and salt, which in great excess may be injurious to health. Modern food technology has allowed us to avoid an excess of nitrate and salt in preserved food. All the preservatives used today are well tested and harmless even in 100 times their concentration in any food. Almost all have stood the test of time and none has ever been linked to any health hazard.

Fast Foods

What exactly are fast foods? It seems that they are bad for you but since no one claims to know what slow foods would be like it is difficult to see what it is that causes the harm. Some of the fastest cooking I have encountered was the cooking of scallops in a wok in China. The actual cooking time was under one minute. They were delicious and seemed to be without any danger to my health. Would they have been better for me if they had been cooked for ten minutes? Fast food is such a meaningless term that one has to question the authority of those who bandy it about as a form of verbal shorthand to conceal their personal dislike of foods such as hamburgers, pizzas and hot dogs. It displays a food snobbery that is so unjustified that it needs to be disguised behind a wall of meaningless jargon.

Reclaimed Meat

Whenever I carve a leg of lamb I feel saddened that I cannot cut decent slices as I get near the bone. Often this meat goes to waste. How much better it would be if it could be 'reclaimed'. It is perfectly good meat. Fortunately, when an animal is butchered, the meat that is left on the carcass, too near the bone, or in too small an area for it to be cut off to make good butcher's meat, can be recovered by high pressure techniques. This meat is termed 'reclaimed meat'. It is perfectly good, healthy protein and has long been presented and eaten as corned beef, Spam and doner kebabs. However, when the same reclaimed meat is used by the food industry for mass catering it becomes an object of disgust. The same people who today sneer at the use of reclaimed meat tell us that in wartime Britain, when Spam and corned beef formed a major part of our protein intake, the population was at its healthiest.

It is clear that there is no such thing as junk food. It is a product of non-scientific pressure groups that, out of ignorance or prejudice, try to persuade us we are on the brink of a health catastrophe. The problem is not with the food we eat, but with the lifestyle of 'junk eaters'.

THREE

Junk Food Companies Do Not Offer Healthy Alternatives

Marion Nestle

> Marion Nestle is a nutrition expert and writes about nutrition for the *San Francisco Chronicle*. In this entry Nestle looks at the marketing trend of "Smart Choices" labeling. Although Smart Choice labels are designed to help consumers find healthy products, Nestle contends that Smart Choice products are seldom healthy. Instead, she believes that the use of Smart Choice labeling is little more than a marketing tool. Unfortunately, she notes, many nutrition experts have supported Smart Choice labeling. Because organizations like the American Heart Association receive money from the food industry, she explains, these organizations have a conflict of interest. Without unbiased experts, Nestle argues, there is no place for the public to find neutral advice on healthy food choices.

Q: Every junk food I pick up looks as if it has a sticker telling me how healthy it is. How do they get away with this?

A: Wait! It's about to get weirder. Soon arriving at a supermarket near you are food packages labeled with Smart Choices logos. These are supposed to guide you to "smarter" food selections.

The program has a philosophical basis: A junk food with a little less sugar, salt, saturated fat or other nutritional evils will be better for you than other junk foods.

I know. Nutritionists are not supposed to call them "junk foods." We are supposed to call them "foods of minimal nutritional value." Whatever we call them, we don't usually recommend them. We advise choosing minimally processed foods with no unnecessary additives.

"Better-for-You" Foods

I also care about how foods are produced and used, so I recommend what the Oakland-based Prevention Institute advises: Choose foods that have been produced safely, fairly, sustainably and humanely, and that are available, accessible and affordable to everyone.

For years now, PepsiCo has put green Smart Spot labels on its "better-for-you" foods and drinks. Kraft has used its equally green Sensible Solutions labels to identify "better-choice" options of Lunchables and macaroni and cheese. You might not be able to tell one Lunchable from another, but Kraft can. Like other companies, it sets up its own nutritional standards. Unsurprisingly, hundreds of its products qualify for its self-determined nutritional criteria.

Where is the Food and Drug Administration [FDA] in all this? Busy elsewhere.

You might wonder what happens if independent experts establish the criteria. This experiment was performed by Hannaford, a supermarket chain in the Northeast. It developed a Guiding Stars program that awards one, two or three stars to qualifying foods. It applied independently determined standards to 27,000 products in its stores.

Oops. Only 23 percent qualified for even one star. Worse, 80 percent of that 23 percent were fresh fruits and vegetables in the produce section. By independent nutritional standards, everything else is a junk food.

Junk Food Marketing

The best way to sell junk foods is to make them appear healthier. The best way to do that is to entice nutrition experts to create easier standards. Enter Smart Choices.

This program is the result of years of food industry consultation with nutrition professionals. It replaces the individual programs of participating companies so you have a "single, trusted and easily recognizable dietary symbol" to help you make "smarter choices within product categories," based on "consensus science." Sounds good, no?

Many critics of junk food say that the Smart Choices program promotes foods that are seldom healthy and that the program is merely a marketing tool.

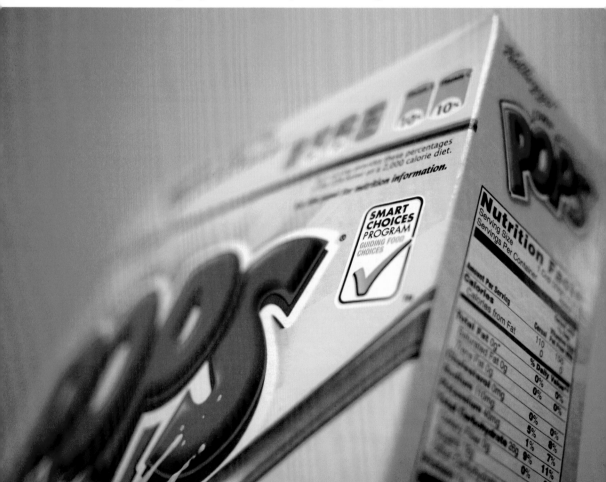

But is a "better-for-you" junk food really a good choice? Of course not. Smart Choices is about marketing, not health.

Its "consensus science" nutritional criteria allow rather generous amounts of sugars and salt so many processed foods can qualify. They reduce the value of food to a few nutrients. The standards do not deal with how foods are produced, how processed they are or how they are used in daily diets.

One underlying purpose of this united program is surely to stave off federal regulations requiring a traffic-light rating system such as that used in England and Australia. Consumers prefer this system to those that use check marks and understand that they can freely choose green-lighted foods but should avoid the red-lighted foods. No wonder food companies don't like it.

Another reason to pre-empt the FDA's proposal to require disclosure of the full number of calories in a package on its front label. Smart Choices lists calories per serving and the number of servings, just as the confusing Nutrition Facts label does now.

The marketing benefits are obvious. Only the health benefits are debatable.

I would dismiss the Smart Choices program as just another food industry marketing ploy except for the involvement of health professionals in its development. Collaborators include organizations such as the American Dietetic Association and the American Heart Association. To my dismay, they also include the American Society of Nutrition [ASN], an organization of nutrition scientists to which I belong. Indeed, the ASN manages the "scientific integrity" of the project. In effect, the ASN is endorsing products that bear the Smart Choices logo.

Conflict of Interest

The ASN is not alone in its financial partnerships with food companies. The American Heart Association endorses sugary breakfast cereals, and the American Dietetic Association allows food companies to sponsor its nutrition information sheets. But the goals of health organizations and of businesses are not the same.

Reading Food Labels 101

This label gives percentages for recommended daily nutritional allowances based on a 2,000-calorie-per-day diet. For example, a label may show that a serving of the food provides 30 percent of the daily recommended amount of fiber. This means you need another 70 percent to meet the recommended goal. Remember this is just an estimate, but it serves as a good guide.

Check the serving size, particularly how many servings there are in the container. If there are two and you eat the whole container, you are eating double the calories that are on the label!

Try to minimize saturated and trans fat. These are both bad fats that clog arteries.

Get enough fiber, vitamins A and C, calcium, and iron.

The less cholesterol and sodium you eat, the better. The latest recommendation for sodium is less than 2,300 mg per day for adults and even less for kids, depending on their age.

Try to keep these low. More sugar means more calories.

Nutrition Facts

Serving Size 1 cup (228g)
Serving Per Container 2

Amount Per Serving

Calories 250   Calories from Fat 110

% Daily Values*

Total Fat 12g	**18%**
Saturated Fat 3g	**15%**
Trans Fat 1.5g	
Cholesterol 30mg	**10%**
Sodium 470mg	**20%**
Total Carbohydrates 1g	**10%**
Dietary Fiber 0g	**0%**
Sugars 5g	

Protein 5g

Vitamin A	4%
Vitamin C	2%
Calcium	20%
Iron	4%

*Percent Daily Values are passed on a 2,000 calorie diet. Your Daily Values may be higher or lower depending on your calories needs.

	Calories	2,000	2,500
Total Fat	Less than	55g	60g
Sat Fat	Less than	20g	25g
Cholesterol	Less than	300mg	300mg
Sodium	Less than	2,400mg	2,400mg
Total Carbohydrates		300g	375g
Dietary Fiber		25g	30g

Taken from: Alliance for a Healthier Generation, William J. Clinton Foundation/American Heart Association. www.healthiergeneration.org.

The partnerships put nutrition professionals in a serious conflict of interest. How can they advise the public about food choices when they are paid to endorse products that many nutritionists would agree are nutritionally inferior? How can they argue that eating a marginally better food product will produce a real health benefit, when so many lifestyle choices are involved?

This is on my mind because I recently received a letter from the ASN nominating me to join the board of directors of the Smart Choices program. I replied that I appreciated the nomination, but think the program ill-advised.

My letter appeared in the society's newsletter along with a response from its executive director: "Rather than seeing this as a conflict of interest, we see ASN as having a responsibility to help consumers make better food choices. ASN is rooted in science and believes that information provided to consumers should be science based. . . . Unfortunately, there is not a sufficient research base to suggest that any dietary guidance program . . . will be effective in improving the health of the population."

My point precisely. If health benefits are uncertain, it makes no sense to endorse food products simply because they meet arbitrary nutritional criteria.

What is at stake here is the integrity of nutrition advice. People constantly ask me whose nutrition advice can be trusted. I am tempted to say, "Mine, of course," but I understand the dilemma. If the most prestigious nutrition and health organizations have financial ties to food companies, how can you trust them to tell you what foods are best to eat?

Smart Choices is coming. Watch for the logos and decide for yourself whether they are useful.

FOUR

Junk Food Is as Addictive as Drugs

Arun Gupta

Arun Gupta is the founding editor of the *Indypendent* newspaper and the author of the forthcoming book *The Decline of the American Empire*. In the following selection Gupta explores the American addiction to junk food. The junk food business, he states, is a multibillion-dollar industry, and junk food is scientifically conditioned to create and satisfy food cravings. Primarily, Gupta writes, junk food relies on three ingredients: salt, sugar, and fat. The junk food industry also relies on a heavily subsidized agricultural industry, he notes, supplying inexpensive produce and meat. Although fast food and junk food companies are able to create profitable products that consumers crave, he believes these companies also create products that are feeding the obesity epidemic. Unless Americans break their dependency on junk food, Gupta argues, their overall health will suffer.

Every chef is said to have a secret junk food craving. For Thomas Keller, chef-owner of Per Se and The French Laundry, two of the most acclaimed restaurants in the country, it's Krispy Kreme Donuts and In-N-Out cheeseburgers. For David Bouley, New York's reigning chef in the '90s, it's "high-quality potato chips."

"Father of American cuisine" James Beard "loved McDonald's fries," while Paul Bocuse, an originator of nouvelle cuisine, once declared McDonald's "are the best French fries I have ever eaten." Masaharu Morimoto is partial to "Philly cheese steaks," and Jean-Georges Vongerichten confesses a weakness for Wendy's spicy chicken sandwich. Other accomplished but less-famous chefs admit to craving everything from Peanut M&Ms, Pringles and Combos to Kettle Chips and Kentucky Fried Chicken [KFC].

Having attended culinary school and cooked professionally, I can wax rhapsodic about epicurean delights such as squab, Beluga caviar, black truffles, porcini mushrooms, Iberico Ham, langoustines, and acres of exceptional vegetables and fruits. But I also have an unabashed junk food craving: Nacho Cheese Doritos. Sure, there are plenty of other junk foods I enjoy, whether it's Ben & Jerry's Ice Cream or Entenmann's baked goods, but Doritos are the one thing I desire and seek out regularly. (Not that I ever have to look that hard; I've encountered them everywhere from rural villages in Guatemala to tiny towns in the Canadian Arctic.)

Junk Food Cravings

For years I wondered why I craved Doritos. I knew the Nacho Cheese powder, which coats your fingers in day-glo orange deliciousness, was one component, as were the fatty, salty chips that crackle and melt into a pleasing mass as you crunch them. I figured there was a dollop of nostalgia in the mix, but an ingredient was still missing in my understanding. Then I read a spate of articles about "umami," designated the fifth taste, along with sweet, sour, salty, and bitter, means "deliciousness" in Japanese, and is described as "a meaty, savory, satisfying taste."

I knew some foods—parmesan cheese, seaweed, shellfish, tomatoes, mushrooms and meats—were high in umami-rich compounds such as glutamate, inosinate and guanylate. (Most people know umami from the much-maligned MSG, or mono sodium glutamate.) And I knew combining various sources of umami—such as the bonito-flake and kombu-seaweed broth known as dashi, the foundational stock of Japanese cuisine—magnified the effect and delivered a uniquely satisfying wallop of flavor.

What I didn't know was that "Nacho-cheese-flavor Doritos, which contain five separate forms of glutamate, may be even richer in umami than the finest kombu dashi (kelp stock) in Japan," according to a *New York Times* article from last year [2008].

Mystery solved. Now I knew that whenever the Doritos bug bit me, I was jonesing for umami. I had to admit it: I am a junk food junkie and Frito-Lay is my pusher-man.

The Junk Food Business

I am hardly alone. Frito-Lay is the snack-food peddler to the world, with over $43 billion in revenue in 2008. The 43-year-old cheesy chip is a "category killer," dominating the tortilla chip market with a 32 percent share in 2006, and number two in the entire U.S. "sweet and savory snacks category," just behind Lay's potato chips.

$1.7 billion in annual sales in the U.S. is big business. Behind the enigma of Doritos' dominance, and the lure of junk food to even the most refined palates in the world, are the wonders of food science. That science, in the service of industrial capitalism, has hooked us on a food system that is destroying our health with obesity-related diseases. And that food system is based on a system of factory farming at one end, which churns out cheap, taxpayer-subsidized commodities like corn, vegetable oil and sweeteners, and the giant food processors at the other, like Frito-Lay, that take these commodities and concoct them into endless forms of addictive junk foods.

Steven Witherly begins his book, *Why Humans Like Junk Food*, by noting in studying the "psychobiology" of Doritos he consumed the "food intake and chemical senses literature—over five hundred research reports and four thousand abstracts— in order to discern the popularity of Doritos." Witherly coined the term "Doritos Effect" to explain its popularity and in his book outlines 14 separate ways in which Doritos appeals to us.

Critics say the combination of nacho cheese powder, fats, salt, and "umami," or "deliciousness," gives Nacho Cheese Doritos an addictive quality.

Junk Food Science

There's the "taste-active components," sugar, salt and umami; ingredients like buttermilk solids, lactic acid, and citric acid that stimulate saliva, creating a "mouth-watering" sensation; the "high dynamic contrast" of powder-coated thin, hard chips that melt in the mouth; a complex flavor aroma; a high level of fat that activates "fat recognition receptors in the mouth . . . increases levels of gut hormones linked to reduction in anxiety . . . activates brain systems for reward, and enhances ingestion for more fat"; toasted, fried corn that triggers our evolutionary predilection for cooked foods; starches that break down quickly, boosting blood levels of insulin and glucose; and so on.

Witherly explains that some umami sources like MSG don't have much taste by themselves, but when you add salt, "the hedonic [highly pleasureable] flavors just explode!" And Doritos has plenty of both. The tiny 2-oz. bag of Doritos I'm holding, which in the past would be a warm-up to a Nacho Cheesier dinner, lists MSG near the top, before "buttermilk solids," along with nearly one-sixth of my recommended daily intake of sodium.

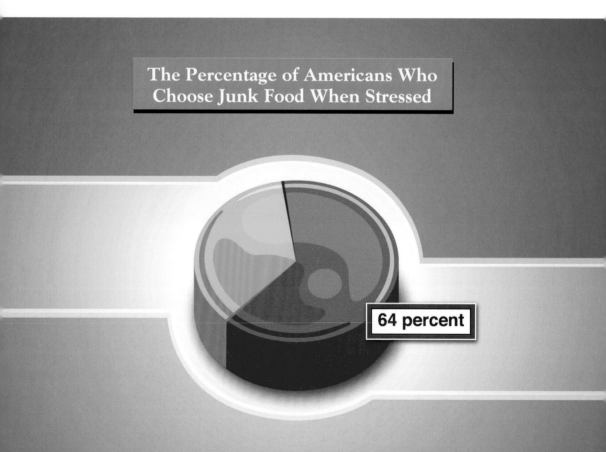

The Percentage of Americans Who Choose Junk Food When Stressed

64 percent

Taken from: Wasa, Satisfaction Survey, February 2009. www.wasacrispbread.com.

One aspect of Doritos that whetted my curiosity was, how much does Frito-Lay spend on goods like corn, oil and cheese? Not surprisingly, this data was nowhere to be found in the annual report of PepsiCo, Frito-Lay's parent company. But I gleaned a clue from a 1991 *New York Times* article. In it, a Wall Street analyst stated that Frito-Lay's profit margin, around 19 percent in those days (which is close to its margin of late), approached that of Kellogg's. The analyst, an expert on the food industry, said: "Kellogg buys corn for 4 cents a pound and sells it for $2 a box." That's a markup of nearly 5,000 percent over the base ingredient.

I'll save you the math, but Frito-Lay may do even better than Kellogg's. If it uses two ounces of cornmeal in my 99 cent bag of Doritos, it apparently costs the snack-food giant less than one measly penny. And here's a critical point about the food industry. The more they can process basic food commodities, the more profits they can gobble up at the expense of farmers. In *The End of Food*, Paul Roberts writes that in the 1950s, farmers received about half the retail price for the finished food product. By 2000, "this farm share had fallen below 20 percent."

Junk Food Agriculture

This is the result of the global food system constructed by the U.S. and other Western powers under the World Trade Organization [WTO]. Countries that once strived for food security by supporting their domestic farmers are now forced—in the name of free trade—to open their agricultural sectors to competition from heavily subsidized Western agribusinesses. By the mid-1990s, according to rural sociologist Philip McMichael, 80 percent of farm subsidies in Western countries went to "the largest 20 percent of (corporate) farms, rendering small farmers increasingly vulnerable to the vicissitudes of a deregulated (and increasingly privately managed) global market for agricultural products."

The WTO-enforced system and government subsidies enables food giants—such as PepsiCo, Kraft, Mars, Coca-Cola, McDonald's, Burger King and Wal-Mart—to source their ingredients globally, giving them the power to force down prices, which drives more and more farmers off the land in the global North and South alike. Then the food companies turn around and manufacture high-profit products that seem like an unbelievable bargain to us. In fact, they make this a selling point, and not just with "Dollar Menus."

Last year, in the wake of the economic meltdown, KFC launched the "10 Dollar Challenge," inviting families to try to re-create a meal of seven pieces of fried chicken, four biscuits and a side for less than its asking price of 10 bucks. Of course this is a virtually impossible feat, apart from dumpster diving. But KFC isn't hawking alfalfa sprouts and a plate of mashed yeast at that price. Witherly, in *Why Humans Like Junk Food*, writes that "high energy density food is associated with high food pleasure." The corporate food's revenue model is based on designing products oozing with fat, salt, sugar, umami and chemical flavors to turn us into addicts.

Fast Food Addiction

While food companies can trot willing doctors, dieticians and nutritionists who claim that eating their brand of poison in moderation can be part of a balanced diet, the companies are like drug dealers who prey on junkies. As Morgan Spurlock explained about McDonald's in *Super Size Me*, the targets are "heavy users," who visit Golden Arches at least once a week and "super heavy users," who visit ten times a month or more. In fact, according to one study, super heavy users "make up approximately 75 percent of McDonald's sales."

Perhaps no company better exemplifies the intersection of factory farming, fast food and food addiction than McDonald's. It pioneered many of the practices of standardized, industrial food production that made it into a global behemoth. In 1966 McDonald's switched from about 175 different suppliers for fresh potatoes to J.R. Simplot Company's frozen French fry. A few years later, McDonald's switched from a similar number of beef suppliers to just five. Within a decade, notes Eric Schlosser [author of *Fast Food Nation*] McDonald's had gone from 725 outlets nationwide to more than 3,000.

Tyson did the same with chicken, which was seen as a healthy alternative to red meat. It teamed up with McDonald's to launch the Chicken McNugget nationwide in 1983. Within one month McDonald's became the number two chicken buyer in the country, behind KFC. The McNugget also transformed chicken processing. Today, Tyson makes most of its money from processed chicken, selling its products to 90 of the 100 largest restaurant chains. As for the health benefits, Chicken McNuggets have twice as much fat per ounce as a hamburger.

The entire food industry, perhaps best described as "eatertainment," has refined the science of taking the cheap commodities pumped out by agribusiness and processing them into foodstuffs that are downright addictive. But food is far more than mere fuel. It is marketed as a salve for our emotional and psychological ills, as a social activity, a cultural outlet and entertainment.

Fat, Salt, and Sugar

Faced with little time to cook bland industrial meat and drawn to exciting and addictive processed foods, most Americans gorge on convenience food. In 1900, the typical American woman spent six hours a day in food prep and cleanup. By last year, Americans on average took 31 minutes a day. For many, "cooking time" consists of opening up takeout containers, dumping the contents on a plate and throwing away the trash.

To get us in the door (or to pick up their product at the supermarket), food companies stoke our gustatory senses. The food has to be visually appealing, have the right feel, texture and smell. And most of all, it has to taste good. To that end, writes David Kessler in *The End of Overeating*, the food industry has honed in on the "three points of the compass"—fat, salt and sugar.

One anonymous food-industry executive told Kessler, "Higher sugar, fat and salt make you want to eat more." The executive admitted food is designed to be "highly hedonic," and that the food industry is "the manipulator of the consumers' minds and desires."

This food is even designed to be pre-digested. Factory-farmed meats are ground up, injected with salt, water, a multitude of flavorings and chemicals, reconstituted and often processed with extra fat (like the McNugget). Speaking to an expert in "sensory stimulation and food," Kessler explains how food is engineered to deliver pleasing flavors, aromatic and textural sensations and dissolve easily in the mouth. He writes: "In the past Americans typically chewed a mouthful of food 25 times before it was ready to be swallowed; now the average American chews only ten times." Even the bolus—the wad of chewed food—is designed to be smooth and even. It's "adult baby food."

Referencing studies with either humans or lab animals, Kessler shows how varying concentrations and combinations of fat and sugar intensify neurochemicals, much the same way cocaine does. One professor of psychiatry explains that people self-administer food in search of "different stimulating and sedating effects," just as is done with a "speedball"—which combines cocaine and heroin.

Sensory Overload

Kessler deconstructs numerous restaurant chain foods to show they are nothing more than layers of fat, salt and sugar. A reoccurring item is "bacon-cheese fries," a coronary event on a plate that displays dazzling engineering precision. One food consultant calls it "cheap filler" in which "20 cents' worth of product gets me $5 worth of wow." The expert in sensory stimulation explains, "Adding more fat gives me more flavor. It gives me more salt. And that bacon gives me a lot more lubricity." A food scientist for Frito-Lay describes the textural appeal: "You've got some pieces that are crispy on the outside, soft on the inside. It's warm. It's probably gooey, stringy, so you have to use your fingers a lot to eat it, and you have to lick your fingers. It's all multisensory."

Or take the McGriddle, which can be deconstructed along the "three points of the compass." It starts with a "cake" made of refined wheat flour, essentially a sugar, pumped with vegetable shortening, three kinds of sugar and salt. This cradles an egg, cheese and bacon topped by another cake. Thus, the McGriddle, from the bottom up, is fat, salt, sugar, fat, then fat and salt in the cheese, fat and salt in the bacon, finished off with fat, salt and sugar. And this doesn't indicate how highly processed the sandwich is. McDonald's bacon, a presumably simple product, lists 18 separate ingredients, including what appear to be six separate sources of umami.

The success of the McGriddle and sandwiches like Wendy's Baconator, which mounds six strips of bacon atop a half-pound cheeseburger and sold 25 million in its first eight weeks, has inspired an arms-race-like escalation among chain restaurants. Burger King has a near-identical imitation with the French Toast Sandwich. In 2004 Hardee's went thermonuclear with its 1,420-calorie, 107-grams-of-fat-laden "Monster Thickburger." And people are gobbling them up.

Junk Food and Disease

Perhaps you feel smug (and nauseated) by all this because you are a vegetarian, a vegan or a locavore, or you only eat organic and artisanal foods. Don't. Americans are under the thrall of the food industry. More than half the population eats fast food at least once a week; 92 percent eat fast food every month; and "Every month about 90 percent of American children between the ages of three and nine visit a McDonald's," states Schlosser.

We know this food is killing us slowly with diabetes, heart disease and cancer. But we can't stop because we are addicts, and the food industry is the pusher. Even if we can completely opt out (which is almost impossible), it's still our land that is being ravaged, our water and air that is being poisoned, our dollars that are subsidizing the destruction, our public health that is at risk from bacterial and viral plagues. Changing our perilous food system means making choices—not to shop for a greener planet, but to collectively dismantle the nexus of factory farming, food corporations and the political system that enables them. It's a tall order, but it's the only option left on the menu.

FIVE

Junk Food Is Not as Addictive as Drugs

Tom Venuto

Tom Venuto is a writer and the author of *The Body Fat Solution*. In this selection Venuto dissects recent research on food addiction. He notes that research on food cravings has led a number of commentators to suggest that junk food is as addictive as drugs. Venuto agrees that cravings for junk food are completely normal, but he does not believe that comparing food to drug addiction is helpful. Although some people develop problems with food, such as binge eating, he notes that there are other studies that show that individuals are able to control food cravings. Instead of blaming our cravings for junk food on addiction, Venuto argues that individuals should be working to control these cravings in practical ways.

The theory of food addiction is getting tons of press lately. I think it's partly because of popular new books like David Kessler's *The End of Overeating*, on top of a whole slew of earlier books about sugar addiction. There has also been a lot of hyped-up media reporting on the latest research, with headlines suggesting that "Junk food is as addictive as heroin" or "Hormones turn hungry people into junkies." I don't believe that food is addictive in the same way that drugs are addictive, but there are definitely some parallels. Drug addiction and food intake involve some of the same neural systems in the brain, so lessons could be learned about certain types of obesity by studying drug addiction research.

The foods most often associated with addiction are sugary, fatty and salty foods. Coincidentally, that combination is what makes food highly palatable and energy dense. It tastes good (so we like it!), which makes it easy to eat a lot of it, which can contribute to obesity.

Some experts have been claiming for years that sugar can be addictive. It's only fairly recently that researchers have studied the brain neurochemistry in a lab controlled situation and come to some somewhat strong conclusions. In 2008, researchers from Princeton University published their findings from a series of rat studies in the *Neuroscience Biobehavior Review*. They concluded:

> Food is not ordinarily like a substance of abuse, but intermittent bingeing and deprivation changes that. Based on the observed behavioral and neurochemical similarities between the effects of intermittent sugar access and drugs of abuse, we suggest that sugar, as common as it is, nonetheless meets the criteria for a substance of abuse and may be "addictive" for some individuals when consumed in a "binge-like" manner. This conclusion is reinforced by the changes in limbic system neurochemistry that are similar for the drugs and for sugar. The effects we observe are smaller in magnitude than those produced by a drug of abuse such as cocaine or morphine. . . . Nonetheless, the extensive series of experiments revealing similarities between sugar-induced and drug-induced behavior and neurochemistry lends credence to the concept of "sugar addiction."

Junk Food Cravings

Most people don't need a new study to tell them that they crave specific foods at times. Cravings and occasional lapses of overeating are a real and persistent challenge to dieters and it's clear that food can be used or even abused for reasons outside of physical

"Comfort food...comfort food...comfort..."

"Comfort food . . . Comfort food . . . Comfort . . .", cartoon by Joseph Farris. www.CartoonStock.com.

hunger and nutrition, for pleasure or to "medicate emotions." Most people would also agree that eating a lot of sugary food can sharpen your sweet tooth so sugar consumption begets more sugar consumption. But is the desire for sugar or comfort foods the same as being addicted to alcohol or even heroin or is that comparison taking it too far?

Even if the way some people consume sugar or junk food meets some of the diagnostic criteria for addiction, it's my belief that it's not beneficial to perpetuate the idea that food is addictive in the same way and magnitude as drugs. I think we should leave it at admitting that we sometimes struggle with overeating—for a wide variety of reasons, only one of which is neurochemical. An important first step in solving any problem is admitting that you have one. But there's a big difference between saying, "I sometimes overeat" and "I am a food addict."

The research is showing that there's definitely something going on chemically and neurologically with dopamine, opioids and the reward and pleasure systems of the brain when sugary or sugary and fatty foods are eaten. Even genetics play a role, leaving some people more susceptible, as some obesity genes appear to act on reward circuitry.

However, there's also research that says you can control food cravings and curb calorie consumption with behavioral and psychological restraint strategies. Obesity is the result of a combination of biology, behavior and environment, not just genetics or a stew of brain chemicals gone awry.

Practicing Moderation

It's important to learn and develop a set of strategies for what to do when you feel cravings. Part of the solution is having some rules about how flexible you'll be in your approach. Somewhat paradoxically, allowing yourself to give in to your cravings is generally more effective than total abstinence, with few exceptions (such as binge eating disorder, etc). That means for the average person, permitting a certain number of free meals each week or setting a compliance rule, and learning how to enjoy your favorite foods—infrequently and in moderation.

It also pays to avoid overly restrictive diets in favor of the slow, steady, moderate approach to weight loss. Crash diets have downsides for anyone but they are an especially bad idea for people susceptible to cravings or addictive-like eating behavior. Periods of deprivation are often followed by the "boomerang" of overeating or bingeing. Eating on a regular schedule, preferably with 5–6 small meals per day, or with healthy pre-planned snacks between meals, is an ideal meal plan for helping to control cravings and decrease hunger.

Stress management strategies are critical. Stress is a major cause of relapse in former drug users and stress can be a prime cause of diet failure and weight regain. The brain centers that regulate appetite are all stress sensitive and one long-standing theory of hunger says that eating comfort foods can become a conditioned response to stress.

Stress management techniques are an effective tool for reducing junk food cravings.

Controlling Your Food Environment

Setting up a social support system and controlling your environment by removing as many triggers and eating cues as possible can help as well. Visual cues alone can trigger a food craving so when someone says, "I can't help myself, I eat everything in sight," part of the solution is contained right within that complaint—get the junk out of your sight.

Granted, that's almost impossible to do completely in our modern society. Being surrounded by temptations and triggers is a major contributor to the obesity problem today. But you do have a remarkable amount of control over your own home and personal environment, so don't make it any worse than it is by keeping junk around. I'm writing this on November 1st. I wonder how many people have leftover candy from Halloween who haven't thrown it away yet.

I also recommend techniques from fields such as Neuro-Linguistic Programming and cognitive psychology. . . . It's possible to literally talk yourself out of inappropriate eating—and by the way, this is one of the many differences between humans and rats, so we should be careful not to read too much into the rodent research.

It's true that there are biological origins of food cravings, so you shouldn't feel weak or guilty about wanting certain foods—it means you're human. What really matters is how you respond to those urges and knowing that ultimately, you are in control.

SIX

Junk Food Should Be Taxed

Paul Michael

Paul Michael is an adman and blogger for Wise Bread. In the following selection Michael suggests that the government should tax junk food just as it taxes alcohol and cigarettes. As with consumer products like liquor, he notes, fast food should be eaten in moderation; but because most Americans choose to gorge themselves on junk food, it should be taxed. The government, Michael believes, could use this money to pay down debt, improve infrastructure, and even to supplement the costs of fresh fruits and vegetables. In essence, he argues, a tax will not prevent people from eating junk food, but a tax on junk food can help provide people with more affordable, healthy options.

Should there be a "fat tax" on junk food?
Yes.

Well, that's just my humble opinion, but I really don't see why this has so many people throwing their arms up in the air with shock. We tax liquor and cigarettes, neither of which are essentials in life. Why not tax something that is bad for our health, preventing more people from buying it and generating much-needed cash in the process?

Taxes on beer, spirits and cigarettes vary from state to state but one thing's for sure—when you grab a shot of your favorite tipple, you're giving money to Uncle Sam. Like most things in life, liquor should be taken in moderation. It's a treat. And as such, we can stomach a little extra money being handed over for our shot of bourbon or pint of ale. (Cigarettes, well, they're a whole different animal and if it weren't for the enormous amount of money they generate they would have been banned years ago. Such is the power of the mighty dollar.)

Similarly, fast food is (or should be) a rare treat, too. Probably more rare than a glass of wine or cold bottle of Bud. If you recall [the documentary] *Super Size Me*, nutritionists interviewed by [director and star] Morgan Spurlock said you should only eat junk food once a month, if at all. That doesn't stop most Americans gorging on fast food like rats in a New York dumpster.

Forbidden Treats

Just look at a few statistics. *In the U.S., 64.5 percent of adults are overweight and 30.5 percent are obese.*

Over half of the population eats fast food once a week with 20 percent eating fast food at least every other day. And high frequency users are more likely to increase fast food consumption because of economic pressure and are attracted to "value" dining options.

It's right there in black and white. The "value" menus are making junk food way too attractive of an option. But what if, as of 2010, every Big Mac, Whopper and "Triple-Bacon Heart Attack Burger" sold in the USA had a $2 fat tax? The money generated would be enormous. We're talking billions and billions of dollars. Even with the decreased consumption due to increased cost, most people would still choose to eat junk food. Maybe not as much, but there are times when the smell of grilled cheese and ground chuck are just irresistible. Now put that fat tax on other junk foods and see the money pile up even more quickly.

People will always want that forbidden treat, and they'll happily pay for it. I don't see anyone complaining about the high price of Belgian chocolate or hand-made English toffee. It's not

The Public Response to Taxing Unhealthy Behaviors

In order to help pay for health care reform and provide coverage for more of the uninsured, would you favor or oppose increasing taxes on items that are thought to be unhealthy, such as soda, alcohol, junk food, and cigarettes?

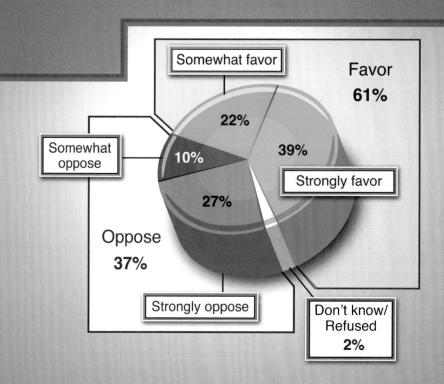

Taken from: Kaiser Family Foundation. www.kff.org.

necessary for survival. It only exists to give people pleasure. And as such, like so many other pleasures in life that are bad for us, we're willing to pay more for them. I know I'd fork over $8 for my junk food of choice, a Chipotle burrito. Right now it's less than $6, but what's $2 more for that one pound of delicious spicy goodness (or badness)?

Subsidizing Healthy Choices

Let the government tax our fatty treats, and let them use that money to pay off some of the debt, or create new jobs, or rebuild the crumbling bridges and infrastructure.

Here's another idea. What if we use the money generated by fast food purchases to subsidize the prices of healthy food, like

Proponents of taxing junk food say that while it may not stop Americans from gorging on fast food, the tax revenue could at least be used to subsidize the prices of fresh fruits and vegetables, which are typically more costly than junk food.

fruits, vegetables and fresh fish? Right now, fast food is generally cheaper than a healthy meal, and much easier to come by. There are fast food restaurants everywhere, but the healthy, cheap and easily accessible options are much more scarce. By channeling the money from junk food to good food, we are not preventing anyone from eating a burger . . . we're just making it way more easy to buy a similarly-priced healthy alternative.

I say the time is right for a fat tax. I know many of you will disagree with me, and that's just one more thing that makes this country great. We can eat our fatty junk foods, we can slurp our sugary sodas, and we can have a good old debate about it all. Now, what's for dessert?

SEVEN

A Food Tax Will Not Decrease Junk Food Consumption

Economist

> In this selection the *Economist* newspaper suggests that a tax on junk food will have little influence on consumption. In theory, the *Economist* states, a tax seems like a good idea; more and more Americans are obese, and obesity leads to higher health costs. Yet even if a tax led to less junk food consumption, the newspaper contends that it still does not solve the problem of which items to tax. Although sugary drinks may be deemed as "junk," the *Economist* observes that other fast and junk food—such as hamburgers—contain needed protein; likewise, a person could eat junk food but not develop a weight problem because of exercise. According to the *Economist*, when all of these factors are considered, taxing junk food is not practical.

Does a tax on junk food make sense?

Economists have long recognised the arguments for imposing special taxes on goods and services whose prices do not reflect the true social cost of their consumption. Such taxes are known as "Pigouvian" after Arthur Pigou, a 20th–century English economist. Environmental taxes are an obvious example. There is also a Pigouvian case for duties on cigarettes, alcohol and gambling.

Smoking increases the risk of cancer for those in the vicinity of the smoker; alcohol abuse and gambling are strongly associated with violence and family breakdown. Moreover, all three habits lead to higher medical costs. In theory governments can make up these costs, or "externalities", with a tax that adjusts the prices people pay to puff, booze or punt. Such a tax might also encourage consumers to live healthier lives.

Support for another such tax, on junk food, is now spreading, especially in America. Congress is considering a tax on sugary drinks to help pay for the planned expansion of health-care coverage. Some analysts would like to see broader duties on junk food. On July 27th [2009] the Urban Institute, a think-tank in Washington, DC, proposed a 10% tax on "fattening food of little nutritional value" that, it claimed, would raise $500 billion over ten years.

The logic for a tax on fattening food may seem obvious. About one-third of Americans are obese, up from 15% in 1980. Fat people are more prone to heart disease, diabetes, bone disorders and cancer. An obese person's annual medical costs are more than $700 greater than those of a comparable thin person. The total medical costs of obesity surpass $200 billion a year in America, which is higher than the bill for smoking. These costs are not all borne by the obese. When health-care costs are shared, obesity becomes a burden for everyone. Thanks to government health-care plans such as Medicare half of America's obesity-related health costs land on taxpayers. In private employer-sponsored health plans the slim pay similar premiums to the overweight.

Will Taxing Junk Food Work?

But would a fat tax affect behaviour? Numerous studies have shown a relationship between the price of food, especially junk food, and body weight. As fast food has become relatively cheaper, so people have become fatter. A new paper from the RAND Corporation, another think-tank, suggests that taxing calories could have a sizeable, if gradual, effect on people's weight. The authors of the study look at changes in the weight and height of

Would a Tax on Junk Food Encourage People to Lose Weight?

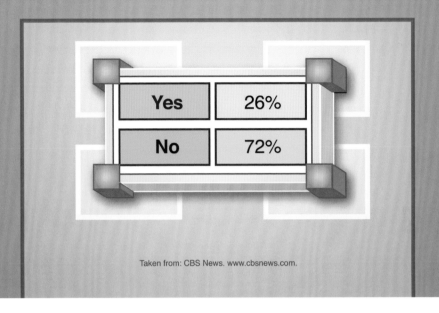

| Yes | 26% |
| No | 72% |

Taken from: CBS News. www.cbsnews.com.

a large group of Americans aged over 50 between 1992 and 2004. They then calculate food-price indices that are skewed towards calorie-dense foods (so a change in the price of butter has more impact than a change in the price of vegetables). By controlling for individual and environmental influences on weight, such as income and health, they then measure whether food-price changes affect body-mass index (BMI). BMI, the ratio of weight in kilograms to the square of height in metres, is a common, if imperfect, gauge of whether someone is over- or underweight.

A person's BMI turns out to be hard to shift in the short term. A 10% increase in the calorie-heavy price index is associated with a small decline, of 0.22, in BMI within two years. But the effects are greater over the longer term. A 10% increase in the price of calories results in a fall in BMI of one to two points over 20 to 30 years. Such a drop would eliminate about half of the observed increase in obesity in America since 1980.

Even so, the idea of tackling obesity via the tax system has some serious flaws. First, there is the question of what to tax. Sugary drinks may not be nutritious, but hamburgers contain some protein along with their fat. More important, junk food is not itself the source of the externality—the medical costs that arise from obesity. Unlike smoking, or excessive gambling and drinking, eating junk food does not directly impair the well-being of anyone else. And because obesity is determined by lack of exercise as well as calorie intake, its ultimate relationship with health costs is more tenuous than that of, say, smoking. It is possible to eat a lot of fatty food, exercise frequently and not generate any externalities. A more direct, though controversial, approach would simply be to tax people on the basis of their weight.

Critics of junk food taxes say that even bacon cheeseburgers have nutritional value and should therefore not be taxed.

A Junk Food Tax Is Unworkable

The distance between junk food and the medical costs of obesity means that a calorie tax could have unintended consequences. A new theoretical paper in the *Journal of Public Economics* even suggests that a tax on junk food could increase obesity, especially among physically active people. If junk food, which is quick and easy to obtain, becomes relatively dearer [costlier], people will spend more time shopping for fresh ingredients and preparing food at home. That could leave less time for exercise.

Even if perverse consequences of this type look improbable, a junk-food tax may have less impact than its advocates expect. New studies on the effect of cigarette and alcohol sin taxes suggest heavy users are less influenced by price changes than others. An analysis of data from the National Longitudinal Study of Adolescent Health shows that American teenagers who smoke more than five cigarettes a day are only one-third as responsive to cigarette prices as lighter smokers. A complementary study of data from America's Health and Retirement Survey shows that alcohol taxes are far less effective for the large minority of heavy drinkers. The biggest consumers of fattening food may prove similarly resilient to price increases, so a fat tax may do little to improve health, at least for today's junk-food addicts. If these same consumers are poorer on average, it would also be regressive. One reason for this is that in some poorer neighbourhoods there may be little fresh food on sale. If junk is all there is, putting up its price will reduce real incomes and make little difference to eating habits and health. Like the foods they aim at, fat taxes look appetising but can have nasty effects.

EIGHT

The Government Should Not Regulate Junk Food

William Saletan

In this selection columnist William Saletan states his belief that there is a cultural war aimed at obesity and the junk food that Americans and others eat. In the past, he notes, reformers had taken aim at tobacco; now they compare junk food to cigarettes. Saletan lists three areas in which the new battle line will be drawn: protecting children, the impact of obesity on health care, and the belief that junk food is not really food. These reformers, however, have one obstacle to overcome, he believes: Whereas no one needs a tobacco product to survive, food—even if it is junk food—is still food. Saletan is the national correspondent at the online magazine *Slate*.

Goodbye, war on smoking. Hello, war on fat.

In a span of two months, smoking bans have been imposed in Scotland, enacted in England, Denmark, and Uruguay, proposed by the government of Portugal, and endorsed by the French public. China has banned new cigarette factories. In Virginia, our third most prolific tobacco state, senators voted to ban smoking in nearly all public places. The Arkansas legislature, backed by a

Republican governor, passed a similar ban and voted to extend this policy to cars in which a child is present. Tobacco companies have won a skirmish here or there, but always in retreat.

The New Enemy—Obesity

So, we've found a new enemy: obesity. Two years ago [in 2004], the government discovered that the targets of previous crusades—booze, sex, guns, and cigarettes—were killing a smaller percentage

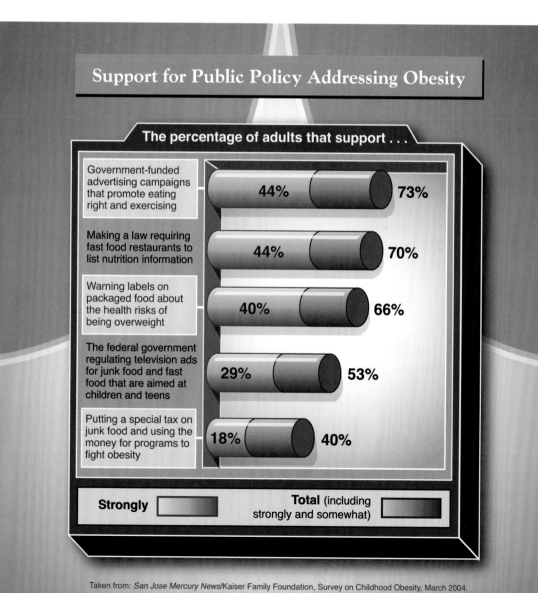

Taken from: *San Jose Mercury News*/Kaiser Family Foundation, Survey on Childhood Obesity, March 2004.

of Americans than they used to. The one thing you're not allowed to do in a culture war is win it, so we searched the mortality data for the next big menace. The answer was as plain as the other chin on your face. Obesity, federal officials told us, would soon surpass tobacco as the chief cause of preventable death. They compared it to the Black Death [a fourteenth-century plague] and the Asian tsunami. They sent a team of "disease detectives" to West Virginia to investigate an obesity outbreak. Last month [March 2006], the surgeon general called obesity "the terror within" and said it would "dwarf 9-11."

How do we fight it? Everyone agrees on exercising and eating responsibly. The debate is over what the government should do. Health advocates want to restrict junk-food sales, regulate advertising, require more explicit labels, and ban trans fats (also known as partially hydrogenated oils), which are often put into crackers, cookies, and other products to prolong shelf life. They marshal the kind of evidence that won the war on smoking: correlations between soda, junk food, obesity, disease, and death. Lawyers who made their fortunes suing tobacco companies are preparing suits against soda companies. Two months ago [in February 2006], when President [George W.] Bush gave a health-care speech at the headquarters of Wendy's, activists compared the hamburger chain to [tobacco giant] Philip Morris. They see themselves as waging the same brave struggle, this time against "the food industry."

But somehow, "the food industry" doesn't sound quite as evil as "the tobacco industry." Something about food—the fact that it keeps us alive, perhaps—makes its purveyors hard to hate. For that matter, the rationale for recent bans on smoking is the injustice of secondhand smoke, and there's no such thing as secondhand obesity. Last year, a Pew Research poll found that 74 percent of Americans viewed tobacco companies unfavorably, but only 39 percent viewed fast-food companies unfavorably. This week, a Pew survey found that more Americans blame obesity, especially their own, on lack of exercise and willpower than on "the kinds of foods marketed at restaurants and grocery stores."

The Battleground Issues

These obstacles don't make the assault on junk food futile. But they do clarify how it will unfold. It will rely on three arguments: First, we should protect kids. Second, fat people are burdening the rest of us. Third, junk food isn't really food.

Targeting kids is a familiar way to impose morals without threatening liberties. You can have a beer or an abortion, but your daughter can't. The conservative aspect of this argument is that you're entitled, as a parent, to decide what your kids can do or buy. That's the pitch Sen. Tom Harkin, D-Iowa, made last week in a bill to crack down on junk food in schools. The liberal half of the argument is that kids are too young to make informed choices. In this case, it's true. Studies show that little kids ask for products they see on television; fail to distinguish ads from programs; and are heavily targeted by companies peddling candy, fast food, and sugared cereal.

This stage of the fat war will be a rout. In schools, the audience is young and captive, and the facts are appalling. According to a government report, 75 percent of high schools, 65 percent of middle schools, and 30 percent of elementary schools have contracts with "beverage"—i.e., soda—companies. The sodas are commonly sold through vending machines. The contracts stipulate how many thousands of cases each district has to buy, and they offer schools a bigger cut of the profits from soda than from juice or water. Soda companies, realizing they're going to lose this fight, are fleeing elementary schools and arguing that high-schoolers are old enough to choose. But health advocates refuse to draw such a line. They're not going to stop with kids.

To keep junk food away from adults, fat-fighters will have to explain why obesity is the government's business. Some say the government created the problem by subsidizing pork, sugar, cream, high-fructose corn syrup, and other crud. Harkin reasons that the government pays for school lunches and must protect this "investment." But their main argument is that obesity inflates health-care costs and hurts the economy through disability and lost productivity. Last month, former President [Bill] Clinton, a confessed overeater, told the nation's governors that obesity has

caused more than a quarter of the rise in health-care costs since 1987 and threatens our economic competitiveness. It's not our dependence on foreign oil that's killing us. It's our dependence on vegetable oil.

Surviving on Junk Food

If the fat-fighters win that argument, they'll reach the final obstacle: the sanctity of food. Food is a basic need and a human right. Marlboros won't keep you alive on a desert island, but Fritos will. To lower junk food to the level of cigarettes, its opponents must persuade you that it isn't really food. They're certainly trying. Soda isn't sustenance, they argue; it's "liquid candy." Crackers aren't baked; they're "engineered," like illegal drugs, to addict people. Last year, New York City's health commissioner asked restaurants to stop using trans fats, which he likened to asbestos. But he ignored saturated fats, which are equally bad and more pervasive. Why are trans fats an easier whipping-cream boy? Because they're mostly artificial.

This, I suspect, is where the war will end. Ban all the creepy-soft processed cookies you want to, but respect nature and nutrition. New York City is purging whole milk from its schools, despite the fact that milk has steadily lost market share to soda during the obesity surge. A fact sheet from Harkin implies that schools should treat milk, French fries, and pizza like soda, jelly beans, and gum. Come on. How many people died in the Irish jelly bean famine? How many babies have nursed on 7-Up? How many food groups does gum share with pizza? If you can't tell the difference, don't tell us what to eat.

NINE

Soft Drinks Are Unhealthy

Michael F. Jacobson

Michael F. Jacobson has a PhD in microbiology and is the cofounder of the Center for Science in the Public Interest. In this selection Jacobson argues that soft drinks negatively impact American health. The increased consumption of soft drinks, he argues, is an important contributing factor to obesity, diabetes, osteoporosis, tooth decay, and heart disease. According to Jacobson, because many Americans have grown up with soft drinks, they consider them both normal and unharmful. In reality, he states, soft drinks are no more than liquid candy, and anyone concerned about his or her health would rarely consume one.

Consumption of carbonated soft drinks in the United States exploded over the past 40 years and has more than doubled since 1971. Those drinks now account for more than one out of every four beverages consumed in America. In 2004, Americans spent $66 billion on carbonated drinks—and billions more on noncarbonated soft drinks. That works out to about $850 per household—enough to buy a computer and year's worth of Internet access. The industry produced enough soda pop that year to provide the average person with 52 gallons—the equivalent of 557 12-ounce servings per year, or 1½ 12-ounce cans per day, for every man, woman, and child. Carbonated soft drinks are the single most-consumed food in the American diet, providing about 7 percent of all calories, according to the government-sponsored 1999–2000 National Health and Nutrition Examination Survey.

The good news is that soft drink consumption has been decreasing. Sales declined by 7 percent from a high of 56.1 gallons per person in 1998 to 52.4 gallons in 2004. Consumption

Americans consume an estimated $850 per household in carbonated drinks annually.

of non-diet sodas declined a remarkable 12 percent. In the first nine months of 2004, the volume of Coca-Cola's products declined by 5 percent. Also, reflecting the increased concern about obesity and consumer interest in low-carb diets, artificially sweetened diet sodas are grabbing a larger share of the market. Diet sodas accounted for 29 percent of total carbonated soft drink sales in 2004, up several percentage points in the last few years and up from just 9 percent in 1970. Given current trends in our overweight nation, in another 10 years diet soda may outsell regular soda.

Most of the data in *Liquid Candy* do not cover sweetened *non*-carbonated beverages—everything from Gatorade to Kool-Aid to Arizona Iced Tea—which are nutritionally equivalent to carbonated beverages. Most of those products contain between 0 and 10 percent fruit juice. If they were included, many of the consumption and sales figures would be significantly higher.

Who Drinks Soda Pop?

Children start drinking soda pop at a remarkably young age, and consumption increases through young adulthood. One-fifth of one- and two-year-old children consume soft drinks. Those toddlers drink an average of seven ounces—nearly one cup—per day. Toddlers' consumption changed little between the late 1970s and mid-1990s.

Almost half of all children between the ages of 6 and 11 drink soda pop, with the average drinker consuming 15 ounces per day. That 1994–96 figure was up slightly from 12 ounces in 1977–78.

The most avid consumers of all are 12- to 29-year-old males. Among teens aged 12 to 19, boys who imbibe soda pop drink an average of almost 2½ 12-ounce sodas (28.5 ounces) per day. One-fourth of 13- to 18-year-old male pop-drinkers drink 2 ½ or more cans per day, and 1 out of 20 drinks 5 cans or more. (Actual intakes probably are higher, because dietary surveys underestimate the quantities of foods people consume, and people may be particularly likely to underestimate foods perceived as being bad for them.)

Daily Beverage Consumption by All Thirteen- to Eighteen-Year-Olds, 1999–2002

Beverage	Boys		Girls		All	
	Ounces	Calories	Ounces	Calories	Ounces	Calories
Carbonated soft drinks, total	25	303	17	194	21	250
Caloric	25	303	16	193	20	249
Diet	1	0	1	0	1	0
Fruit drinks	5	60	5	61	5	60
Caloric carbonated + fruit drinks	29	363	21	254	25	310
All carbonated + fruit drinks	30	363	22	254	26	310
Milk	11	160	7	98	9	130

Taken from: Michael F. Jacobson, *Liquid Candy: How Soft Drinks Are Harming America's Health*, Center for Science in the Public Interest, June 2005.

Teenage girls also drink large amounts of soda pop. Girls who drink soft drinks consume about 1.7 12-ounce sodas per day. One-fourth of 13- to 18-year-old female pop-drinkers drink two or more cans per day, and 1 out of 20 drinks three cans or more. (Women in their 20s average slightly more: two 12-ounce sodas per day.)

By contrast, 20 years earlier, the typical (50th percentile) 13- to 18-year-old consumer (boys and girls together) of soft drinks drank three-quarters of a can per day, while the 95th percentile teen drank 2¼ cans. That's slightly more than one-half of current consumption.

Serving Size

One reason for that increased consumption is that the industry has steadily increased container sizes. In the 1950s, Coca-Cola's 6½-ounce bottle was the standard serving. That grew into the 12-ounce can, and now *that* is being supplanted by 20-ounce bottles (and such gargantuan products as the 64-ounce Double Gulp at 7-Eleven stores). The larger the container, the more soda people are likely to drink, especially when they assume they are buying single-serving containers.

Pricing practices also encourage people to drink large servings. For instance, at McDonald's restaurants a 16-ounce ("small") drink costs about $1.05, while a drink 100 percent larger (a 32-ounce "large") costs only 50 percent more (about $1.57). At a multiplex theater in Maryland, a 16-ounce drink costs $3.25, while the 44-ounce drink, which is 175 percent larger, costs only 30 percent more ($4.25). . . .

The Health Impact of Soft Drinks

The soft drink industry has consistently portrayed its products as being positively healthful, saying they are 90 percent water and contain sugars found in nature. A poster that the National Soft Drink Association (now the American Beverage Association) once provided to teachers stated: "As refreshing sources of needed liquids and energy, soft drinks represent a positive addition to a well-balanced diet. . . . These same three sugars also occur naturally, for example, in fruits. . . . In your body it makes no difference whether the sugar is from a soft drink or a peach."

Currently, in a desperate attempt to link soft drinks to good health, the industry emphasizes that soda contains water, an essential nutrient: "Drink plenty of fluids: consume at least eight glasses of fluids daily, even more when you exercise. A variety of beverages, including soft drinks, can contribute to proper hydration." A similar claim was made in 1998 by M. Douglas Ivester, then Coca-Cola's chairman and CEO [chief executive officer], when he defended the marketing of soft drinks in Africa. He said, "Actually, our product is quite healthy. Fluid replenishment is a key to health. . . . Coca-Cola does a great service because it encourages people to take in more and more liquids."

In fact, soft drinks pose health risks both because of what they *contain* (extra calories, sugar, and various additives) and what they *replace in the diet* (beverages and foods that provide vitamins, minerals, and other nutrients).

Obesity and Soft Drinks

Being overweight or obese increases the risk of diabetes, heart disease, stroke, cancer, and other diseases and causes severe social and psychological problems in millions of Americans. Between 1971–74 and 1999–2002, overweight rates in teenagers soared from 6 percent to 16 percent. What used to be called adult-onset diabetes is now called type 2 diabetes, because the disease is being seen increasingly in teens.

Among adults, between 1976–80 and 1999–2002, the rate of obesity more than doubled, rising from 15 to 31 percent. The overall rates of obesity plus overweight were 47 percent in 1976–80 and 65 percent in 1999–2002.

Numerous factors—from lack of exercise to eating too many calories to genetics—contribute to obesity. Soda pop adds unnecessary, non-nutritious calories to the diet. Nutritionists and weight-loss experts routinely advise overweight individuals to consume fewer calories, especially from such nutrient-free foods as soft drinks. The National Institutes of Health recommends that people who are trying to lose weight or control their weight should drink water instead of sugar-containing soft drinks. . . .

Bones and Osteoporosis

People who drink soft drinks instead of milk or other dairy products likely will have lower calcium intakes. Low calcium intake contributes to osteoporosis, a disease leading to fragile and broken bones. In 2002, the National Osteoporosis Foundation estimated that 10 million Americans had osteoporosis. Another 34 million had low bone mass and were at increased risk for the disease. Women are more frequently affected than men. Considering the low calcium intake of today's teenage girls, osteoporosis likely will continue to be a problem.

The risk of osteoporosis depends in part on how much bone mass is built up early in life. Girls build 92 percent of their bone mass by age 18, but if they don't consume enough calcium in their teenage years they cannot catch up later. That's why experts recommend higher calcium intakes for youths aged 9 to 18 than for adults aged 19 to 50. Teenage girls in 1994–96 were consuming only 60 percent of the recommended amount of calcium; those who drank soft drinks consumed almost one-fifth less calcium than those who didn't drink soft drinks.

Although osteoporosis takes decades to develop, preliminary research suggests that the lower calcium intake that may result from drinking soda pop instead of milk can contribute to broken bones in children. In a study of 200 girls 3 to 15 years old, the 100 who had suffered broken bones had lower bone density than the 100 who had not. In a Mayo Clinic study, researchers looked at rates of bone fracture in residents under the age of 35 in Rochester, Minnesota. They found a 32 percent increase between 1969–71 and 1999–2001 in distal forearm bone fractures in males and a 56 percent increase in females. Among 10- to 14-year-olds of both sexes, the increase was 63 percent. That study couldn't establish a cause-and-effect relationship, but the researchers suggested that increasing obesity rates, increased soft drink and decreased milk consumption, and suboptimal calcium consumption could be the culprits. . . .

Tooth Decay and Erosion

Refined sugars are one of several important factors that promote tooth decay (dental caries). Regular soft drinks promote caries because they bathe the teeth of frequent consumers in sugar-water for long periods of time during the day. An analysis of data from 1971–74 found a strong association between the frequency of between-meal consumption of soda pop and caries. (Those researchers distinguished the effects of soft drinks from sugary desserts.) A recent large study of young children in Iowa found "intake of regular soda pop was the strongest predictor of the extent of caries."

Tooth-decay rates in the United States have declined considerably in recent decades, thanks to such preventive factors as fluoride-containing toothpaste, fluoridated water, and tooth sealants. That may be why one study that used data from 1988–94 found an association between soda consumption and caries in people over 25, but not in younger people. Also, as Amid Ismail, a professor of epidemiology at the University of Michigan's School of Dentistry, points out, Americans consume so many sugary foods it simply may not be possible to tease out the effects of individual foods on teeth.

Caries remains a problem, however, especially for low-income and minority children. As a report from the Surgeon General stated, "Despite recent declines, dental caries is a prevalent disease, with some age and population groups particularly vulnerable." A large survey in California found that children (ages 6–8 and 15) of less-educated parents have 20 percent higher rates of decayed and filled teeth. A national study found that African American and Mexican American children (6 to 18 years old) are about twice as likely to have untreated caries as their white counterparts.

To prevent tooth decay, health experts—and Refreshments Canada (formerly the Canadian Soft Drink Association)—recommend eating sugary foods and beverages with meals and limiting between-meal snacking of sugary and starchy foods. Unfortunately, many heavy drinkers of soft drinks ignore both of those precepts. . . .

Heart Disease

Heart disease is the nation's number-one killer. Some of the most important causes are diets high in saturated and *trans* fats and cholesterol, cigarette smoking, and a sedentary lifestyle. In many adults, a diet high in sugar may also be a modest contributor to heart disease.

High-sugar diets may contribute to heart disease in people who are "insulin resistant" or have "syndrome X." Those people, an estimated one-fourth of adults, frequently have high levels of triglycerides and low levels of HDL ("good") cholesterol in their blood, abdominal obesity, and elevated blood pressure and blood sugar. When they eat a diet high in carbohydrates, their triglyceride and insulin levels rise. In many studies, sugar has a greater effect than other carbohydrates. High triglyceride levels are associated with a higher risk of heart disease and diabetes.

A study of young adults (19 to 38 years old) in Louisiana found a strong association between consumption of sweetened beverages and risk factors for syndrome X. According to the researchers, that finding was not simply due to the subjects consuming excess calories or being overweight.

It is sensible for insulin-resistant people, in particular, to consume low levels of regular soft drinks and other sugary foods, though researchers are urging that everyone reduce their intake of refined carbohydrates. More research is needed on insulin resistance in adolescents.

Kidney Stones

Kidney stones are one of the most painful disorders to afflict humans and one of the most common disorders of the urinary tract. According to the National Institute of Diabetes and Digestive and Kidney Diseases (NIDDK), a unit of the National Institutes of Health, more than 1 million cases of kidney stones were diagnosed in 1996. NIDDK estimates that 10 percent of all Americans will have a kidney stone during their lifetime. Several times more men, frequently between the ages of 20 and 40, are affected than women. Young men are also the heaviest consumers of soft drinks. After a study suggested a link between soft drinks and kidney stones, researchers conducted an intervention trial. That trial involved 1,009 men who had suffered kidney stones and drank at least $5^1/_3$ ounces of soda pop per day. Half the men were asked to refrain from drinking pop, while the others were not asked to do so. Over the next three years, cola drinkers who reduced their consumption (to less than half their customary levels) were almost one-third less likely to experience recurrence of stones. Among those who usually drank fruit-flavored soft drinks—which are acidified with citric acid rather than the phosphoric acid used in colas—drinking less had no effect.

Coming at the problem from another angle, researchers had subjects consume large volumes of cola drinks for one or several days. The next day, the subjects' urine contained higher levels of oxalate and lower levels of magnesium and citrate, changes that could contribute to kidney stone formation. While more research needs to be done to prove the cola-stone connection, NIDDK recommends that people trying to avoid more stones should limit their consumption of cola beverages, as well as of coffee and tea. . . .

Recommendations for Action

Soft drinks are popular, in part, because people like their taste. But powerful advertising, universal availability, low price, and the use of a mildly addictive ingredient (caffeine) are other factors that have made soft drinks a routine snack and a standard component of meals instead of the occasional treat they were considered several decades ago. Moreover, many of today's younger parents grew up with soft drinks, see it as normal to drink pop throughout the day, and so make little effort to restrict their children's consumption.

The bottom line is health. Soft drinks provide enormous amounts of refined sugars and calories to a nation that already does not meet national dietary goals and is experiencing an epidemic of obesity. The replacement of milk by soft drinks in teenage girls' diets may increase rates of osteoporosis. Soft drinks may also contribute to dental problems, kidney stones, and heart disease. Additives in some of the drinks may cause insomnia, behavioral problems, allergic reactions, and cancer.

Based on its past record, the soft drink industry will do everything possible to persuade even more consumers to drink even more soda pop even more often. Parents and health officials need to recognize soft drinks for what they are—*liquid candy*—and do everything they can to return those beverages to their former role as an occasional treat. As Walter Willett, chairman of the nutrition department at the Harvard School of Public Health and overseer of the Nurses' Health Study, said, "The message is: Anyone who cares about their health or the health of their family would not consume these beverages."

TEN

Soft Drinks Are No More Unhealthy than Juice

Karen Kaplan

> Karen Kaplan writes for the *Los Angeles Times* and is co-author of *The Biggest Loser Cookbook*. In this selection Kaplan reports the views of several health experts who suggest that fruit juice is as bad for one's health as soft drinks. Citrus growers developed juice in the early 1900s as a way of processing excess fruit. Although fruit juice has been marketed as a healthy drink, Kaplan notes that many experts believe fruit juice is little more than sugar water. Like soft drinks, she reports, juice may be partly responsible for the current obesity epidemic; likewise, the concentrated levels of sugar in juice may be bad for the liver. Despite these warnings, Kaplan states, the general belief that juice is a healthy beverage remains.

To many people, it's a health food. To others, it's simply soda in disguise.

That virtuous glass of juice is feeling the squeeze as doctors, scientists and public health authorities step up their efforts to reduce the nation's girth. . . .

It's an awkward issue for the schools that peddle fruit juice in their cafeterias and vending machines. It's uncomfortable for advocates of a junk-food tax who say they can't afford to target juice and alienate its legions of fans. It's confusing for consumers who think they're doing something good when they chug their morning OJ [orange juice], sip 22-ounce smoothies or pack apple juice in their children's lunches.

The inconvenient truth, many experts say, is that 100% fruit juice poses the same obesity-related health risks as Coke, Pepsi and other widely vilified beverages.

Juice Does Not Deserve Its Wholesome Image

With so much focus on the outsized role that sugary drinks play in the country's collective weight gain—and the accompanying rise in conditions including diabetes, heart disease and cancer—it's time juice lost its wholesome image, these experts say.

Ounce per ounce, fruit juices contain more calories than nondiet soda, and both contribute to obesity.

"It's pretty much the same as sugar water," said Dr. Charles Billington, an appetite researcher at the University of Minnesota. In the modern diet, "there's no need for any juice at all."

A glass of juice concentrates all the sugar from several pieces of fruit. Ounce per ounce, it contains more calories than soda, though it tends to be consumed in smaller servings. A cup of orange juice has 112 calories, apple juice has 114, and grape juice packs 152, according to the U.S. Department of Agriculture. The same amount of Coke has 97 calories, and Pepsi has 100.

And just like soft drinks, juice is rich in fructose—the simple sugar that does the most to make food sweet.

UC [University of California] Davis scientist Kimber Stanhope has found that consuming high levels of fructose increases risk factors for heart disease and Type 2 diabetes because it is converted into fat by the liver more readily than glucose. Her studies suggest that it doesn't matter whether the fructose is from soda or juice.

"Both are going to promote equal weight gain," she said, adding that she's perplexed by the fixation on the evils of sugar-sweetened beverages: "Why are they the only culprit?"

The History of Juice

Juice is a relatively recent addition to the human diet. For thousands of years, people ate fruit and drank mostly water.

But in the early 1900s, citrus growers in Florida were harvesting more oranges than they could sell. Then they had an epiphany: promote juice.

"You consume more oranges if you drink them than if you eat them whole," said Alissa Hamilton, author of the book *Squeezed: What You Don't Know About Orange Juice*.

The U.S. Army was instrumental in turning orange juice into a commercial product.

It originally served a powdered lemonade to ensure soldiers got enough vitamin C, but it tasted "like battery acid," Hamilton said. So, during World War II, the Army commissioned scientists to invent a system for freezing OJ in a concentrated form. The patent wound up with Minute Maid, which sold cans of frozen juice concentrate in grocery stores.

In the 1950s, pasteurization technology developed by Tropicana made orange juice even more consumer-friendly because it could be sold ready to drink in cartons, like milk.

TV fitness pioneer Jack LaLanne and other health experts touted juice as a natural medicine, and decades of advertising helped secure its place at the breakfast table. Today, roughly half of all Americans consume juice regularly, according to NPD Group, a market research firm.

The Juice Products Assn. emphasizes the value of the vitamins, minerals and phytonutrients in juice, especially when so many Americans eat so little fresh produce.

"If someone can add a glass of fruit juice at breakfast, that's an important addition to the diet," said Sarah Wally, a dietitian for the trade group.

But scientists are increasingly questioning whether the benefits outweigh the sugar and calories that come with them. "The upside of juice consumption is so infinitesimal compared to the downside that we shouldn't even be having this discussion," said Dr. Robert Lustig, a pediatric endocrinologist at UC San Francisco.

Juice and Obesity

Researchers haven't published head-to-head comparisons of how juice and soda contribute to weight gain, but there is evidence that high juice consumption increases the risk of becoming overweight or obese, especially among kids.

One of the earliest studies, in 1997, examined 168 preschool-age children in upstate New York. Kids who drank at least 12 ounces of juice a day were 3 1/2 times more likely than other kids to exceed the 90th percentile for body mass index, qualifying them as overweight or obese.

A 2006 study of 971 low-income youngsters found that each extra glass of juice a day caused children who were already overweight or obese to gain an extra pound each year.

The link between juice and weight gain isn't always found, however. In a 2008 review of 21 studies, six supported the connection and 15 did not.

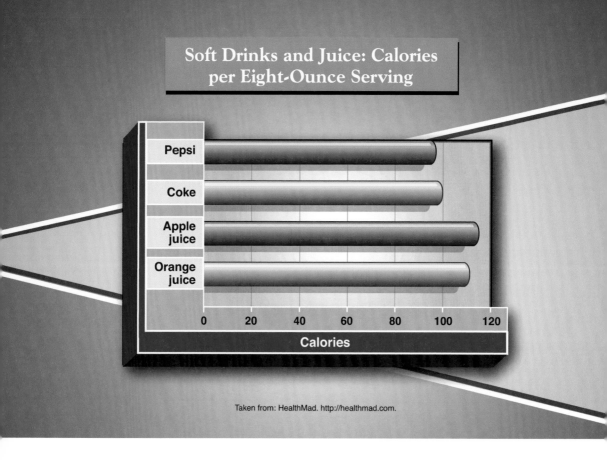

Soft Drinks and Juice: Calories per Eight-Ounce Serving

Pepsi

Coke

Apple juice

Orange juice

Calories

0   20   40   60   80   100   120

Taken from: HealthMad. http://healthmad.com.

In fact, several researchers have linked juice to healthier diets and lower weights. A 2008 report of 3,618 children ages 2 to 11 found that kids who drank at least 6 ounces of juice a day consumed less fat and more vitamins and minerals than kids who drank no juice at all.

But many experts say the data simply reflect a correlation between juice and healthful diets, not a causal relationship.

"Kids who drink more juice are more likely to be eating breakfast, and kids who eat breakfast tend to weigh less than kids who don't," said Kelly Brownell, director of the Rudd Center for Food Policy and Obesity at Yale University.

There's also concern that children who drink lots of sweet beverages such as juice will develop a lifelong preference for sweeter foods. A 2004 Dutch study found that 8- to 10-year-olds preferred sweeter drinks after consuming a sugary orangeade for eight days. They also drank more of it as they acclimated to its sweet taste.

Doctors and health officials have been persuaded to de-emphasize juice in recent years.

The American Academy of Pediatrics' nutrition committee revised its policy in 2001 to recommend that children ages 1 to 6 drink no more than one 4- to 6-ounce serving of juice a day and older kids have no more than two.

"Because juice is viewed as nutritious, limits on consumption are not usually set by parents," the committee wrote in "The Use and Misuse of Fruit Juice in Pediatrics." "Like soda, it can contribute to energy imbalance," causing the weight gain that leads to obesity.

The government's 2005 dietary guidelines recognize that juices can be good sources of potassium, but recommend whole fruit for the majority of daily fruit servings to ensure adequate intake of fiber.

In October [2009], the federal Special Supplemental Nutrition Program for Women, Infants and Children introduced vouchers for fresh produce and reduced the juice allowance. That's a change Billington and his colleagues in the Minnesota Medical Assn. had been pushing for since 2006.

"Having apple juice and eating an apple are not the same," he said.

Juice and Concentrated Sugar

Indeed, as scientists zero in on the causes of rising obesity rates, sugary drinks have emerged as a primary culprit.

Calories consumed in liquid form don't give stomachs the same satisfied feeling as calories eaten in food. People offset an afternoon snack by eating less at dinner, but they don't do that with beverages.

"The studies are pretty clear," said Dr. Barbara Dennison, a research and policy director at the New York State Department of Health in Albany. "You just don't compensate for those calories."

Making matters worse, the human body is ill-equipped to process the sugar that is concentrated in a glass of juice.

When fructose is eaten in a piece of fruit, it enters the body slowly so the liver has time to convert it into chemical energy. But a single glass of apple juice has the fructose of six apples.

"If you overdose on fructose in a liquid, the liver gets overwhelmed," Lustig said. As a result, he said, the fructose turns to fat. "Eating fruit is fine. Drinking juice is not."

Still, the halo surrounding juice remains strong.

As soda is singled out for its role in the rise of obesity, juice is offered as the sensible alternative. In Los Angeles and elsewhere, it is taking the place of soft drinks in school vending machines alongside water and milk.

Brownell of Yale has waged a high-profile campaign to fight obesity with "sin" taxes on soda and other sugary drinks. It's already an uphill battle, and he said he's loath to provoke the tens of millions of Americans who consider their morning juice sacrosanct [sacred].

Dr. Frank Greer, who spent 10 years on the American Academy of Pediatrics' nutrition committee, said he "can't imagine" the group would ever downgrade juice to the status of soda.

"It's such a normal part of the American diet," Greer said. "A glass of fresh-squeezed orange juice for breakfast, my goodness!"

ELEVEN

The National School Lunch Program Is Flawed and Contributes to Junk Food in Schools

Adam Bornstein

Adam Bornstein is a columnist for *Men's Health*. In this selection Bornstein explores a simple question: If junk food is bad for children's health, then why is it available in schools? Although he notes that the National School Lunch Program focuses on nutrition, the program costs schools more money than the federal reimbursement. One method for schools to close this financial gap is to operate vending machines that sell junk food. Falling school budgets and higher prices have made the prospect of healthier cafeteria food even less likely. Many schools are attempting to make healthier choices available, Bornstein notes, but federal regulation may be needed to resolve the problem. Furthermore, Bornstein states that more nutrition education should be required in schools.

It's no secret that childhood obesity is a major problem in America's schools. What's so baffling, though, is that despite our awareness, it's a growing problem. After all, one solution seems obvious and simple: Pull the plug on vending machines,

Adam Bornstein, "Are Schools Selling Junk Food to Kids?" *Men's Health,* November 2008.

ban junk food on campuses, and serve only healthy fare in cafeterias. Case closed, right? If only it were that easy.

"The government system is forcing our schools to choose," says Katie Wilson, Ph.D., president of the School Nutrition Association, a nonprofit organization dedicated to improving school meals and nutrition. "Schools can either provide only healthy foods and go into debt, or allow unhealthy options, which generate revenue but are also a contributing factor to weight gain."

This unappetizing proposition, says Wilson, is the result of education budget cuts and a flawed system. But while it may be hard to swallow, it's just one piece of the puzzle. That's because, well, french fries taste good. So do candy bars, potato chips, and soda. "Unless kids are properly educated, they're going to choose junk over healthy food at school and at home," says Wilson. "Unfortunately, the number one question children ask me about nutrition is, 'Why don't schools teach us right from wrong?'"

We wondered that, too. We also wanted to know how, exactly, a system meant to help kids is ultimately making them fat.

The School Lunch Program

As odd as it sounds, one of the key contributors to poor nutrition in schools—at least indirectly—may be the National School Lunch Program (NSLP). Established in 1946, this federally subsidized program provides calorie-balanced meals at cost to all children, or at reduced or no cost to children in low-income families. The intention, of course, is to give every child access to an inexpensive, healthy lunch. And to ensure that this goal is met, the USDA [U.S. Department of Agriculture] has set these basic nutrition standards for schools to follow.

All meals must provide one-third of the Recommended Dietary Allowance (RDA) for calories, protein, vitamin A, vitamin C, iron, and calcium. This makes sense, considering that children consume 19 percent to 50 percent of their daily calories in the school cafeteria, according to the USDA.

The meals must also match the USDA's Dietary Guidelines for Americans, which limit the fat content of a meal to 30 percent of total calories and cap saturated fat at less than 10 percent.

The program forbids foods of "minimum nutritional value" from being served inside the school cafeteria at mealtimes. These are items that provide less than 5 percent of eight specific nutrients— i.e., "empty-calorie" foods such as gum, soda, and jelly beans, which are primarily sugar.

Loopholes in the System

All of which sounds sensible, but plenty of loopholes exist, particularly in that last requirement: Turns out, foods of minimum nutritional value, while not allowed for sale in the cafeteria, can be sold anywhere else in the school—for instance, from a vending machine on the way to the lunchroom. What's more, candy bars, chips, and doughnuts actually avoid the foods-of-minimum-value designation. (A main ingredient in many of these foods is refined flour, which by federal law is fortified with vitamins and minerals.) As a result, they can be sold in the lunchroom, side by side with healthier options. Of course, that's only if the schools choose to do so. And that leads to the bigger issue: dollars and cents.

"Schools lose money every day because it costs more money to prepare meals than the reimbursement they get from the federal government," says Donald Schumacher, M.D., medical director for the Center for Nutrition and Preventive Medicine, in Charlotte, North Carolina. Case in point: In 2008, the government increased the NSLP subsidy to schools, to $2.57 per meal per student, but the cost to prepare the lunches rose to $2.88. And while schools that purchase foods directly from the USDA receive an additional 20 cents per meal, they're still at an 11-cent deficit.

That amount might seem trivial, but multiply it by the 29.6 million children participating in the NSLP and it comes out to a daily nationwide deficit of $3.2 million. For perspective, a middle school with 1,000 students would be $19,800 in the hole after just 1 year.

Critics say the National School Lunch Program standards are so costly that schools have turned to junk food vending machines to reduce costs.

Schools can raise prices, of course, and some are being forced to do so. But Wilson says this strategy leads to other problems: It defeats the purpose of providing low-cost, healthy meals in the first place, and it can also result in fewer kids purchasing the nutritionally balanced lunches.

The upshot is that schools have instead turned to offering "competitive foods." These items aren't part of the NSLP. They include foods of minimal nutrition—which can be sold in vending machines, school stores, and snack bars—as well as foods that don't meet other USDA guidelines but that can be offered a la carte in the cafeteria. This is where the trouble really begins.

For instance, students buy competitive foods in greater proportions than the USDA-approved meals, taking away from their consumption of fruits and vegetables, according to a report to Congress presented by the Center for Science in the Public Interest. So while the NSLP helps schools serve healthy food, it has also opened the door to options that undermine that effort.

"Without full funding from the government, schools are being pinched, and we need a quick way to make money," says Wilson. "That's why we have vending machines. That's why we sell a la carte. And that's why we purchase unhealthy foods along with healthy foods. They're cheaper than the healthier foods, and we can turn a greater profit."

The Price of a Child's Health

With 71 schools and 64,000 students, Volusia County, Florida, is one of the largest school districts in the country. And when it comes to instituting nutrition reform, it's also one of the most progressive. "Schools have a responsibility to address healthy eating and fitness," says district superintendent Margaret Smith. "And we're determined to protect the health of our students."

So despite a crisis that has forced the closing of several schools, Smith's district has instituted policies to ensure that fresh fruit, vegetables, and whole grains are offered in all schools on a regular basis. At the elementary level, signs are placed throughout cafeterias encouraging students to make healthy food choices, and water is placed at eye level in vending machines to compete with sports drinks. Soda is permitted only in high schools and only after the lunch hour is over. And this year, one school in the district, Pierson Elementary, was among 43 schools nationally recognized for their promotion of healthy initiatives.

But Volusia administrators openly admit that the problems haven't been eliminated entirely. For example, some high-school students still have easy access to vending machines throughout the buildings after lunch is over. "Vending machines provide revenue that helps fund extracurricular activities for students," says Joan Young, the school district's director of cafeteria services.

This is one way the district manages to keep athletic programs afloat in the midst of big budget cuts.

And while healthy dishes are readily available in Volusia schools, the cafeteria also stocks what many teenagers would consider more desirable options, including chocolate cake, cookies, and pizza.

Unhealthy Food Costs Less

But remember, Volusia is working hard to fix these flaws. Many school districts across the country aren't so proactive. And all of these issues are compounded by the soaring cost of food due to high oil prices and a weak dollar. "I've been working in the food industry for 30 years and I've never seen price increases like the ones we've experienced over the past 18 months," says Bob Bloomer, regional vice president of Chartwells-Thompson, a subsidy of Compass Group, the largest food distributor in the world.

Even small price fluctuations can have a major impact: A five-cent increase in the price of milk will cost the Volusia school district an additional $750,000 in the 2008–2009 school year. And Young has especially noticed price increases for the so-called healthiest items, such as whole-wheat bread and products with less sugar.

"The minute you say 'healthy,' it costs more," says Bloomer. "When you say 'zero trans fat,' it costs more. It's the nature of the beast." In Albany County School District 1 in Laramie, Wyoming, margarine with no trans fat costs 262 percent more than the option with trans fat, leading the schools to use the less healthy version. "There are some districts that just don't have the money. They don't care about whole wheat. They don't care about trans fat. And when I say they don't care, I mean they just can't afford it," says Bloomer.

In the end, superintendents and the school board are left with a dilemma: Find new ways to raise millions of dollars, or buy the types of foods students will purchase. "School administrators know that foods of minimum nutritional value provide a profit margin that makes up for what they're losing from the federally

How Often Do You Buy Junk Food at School?

Asked of U.S. teens aged thirteen to seventeen

Frequency	Soda	Candy	Chips/ other snacks
Once a day or more often	15%	8%	12%
A few times a week	28%	20%	26%
A few times a month	14%	19%	22%
Rarely	29%	36%	28%
Never	14%	17%	12%

Percentage of Students

Taken from: Gallup Poll, www.gallup.com.

mandated meal," says Dr. Schumacher. "And these products can even give them a little bit of profit to put back into the school. Where is their incentive to stop that?"

"Education Is Our Fat Burner"

Make no mistake: Many schools are trying, according to the School Nutrition Association. In fact, 71 percent of them have attempted to make a "significant" effort to offer healthy food choices on their menus. And several states now ban vending machines in elementary schools or limit what can be sold in the machines and when students can access them. But clearly, it's going to take sweeping national reform to repair this problem.

New legislation is a good place to start, says Dr. Schumacher. He's working hard to push a bill, HR 1363, that will hopefully help build momentum for improving children's nutrition in schools nationwide. The proposal is an update to the Child Nutrition Act of 1966. It uses current nutrition science to rewrite the definition of foods of minimum nutritional value and requires that they be removed from schools, effectively eliminating a multitude of unhealthy options. "The issue isn't about removing children's ability to make choices, it's about providing healthy options and making it harder for them to access bad foods," says Dr. Schumacher.

Research has shown that this strategy, along with education, can help. In a recent Temple University study of grades four through six, researchers removed all sodas, sweetened drinks, and snacks that didn't meet USDA nutrition standards from vending machines and cafeteria lines in five Philadelphia schools. They also implemented 50 hours of nutrition education for students and encouraged parents to purchase healthy snacks for their kids to eat at home. After 2 years, half as many of these kids became overweight, compared with kids in similar schools without the program.

While those numbers are encouraging, they also underscore the daunting challenge of overcoming childhood obesity. Sure, the study results sound impressive. But some of that is nifty data-crunching—7.5 percent of the children in the prevention program packed on too many pounds, compared with 15 percent of the group that made no changes. Still, we have to start somewhere. And there's little doubt that a combination of approaches is necessary. "If you don't teach kids what's good and what's bad, you don't solve a whole lot by restricting things," says Wilson. "Education is our fat burner."

Nutrition Education

One barrier is the No Child Left Behind Act. Designed to improve the quality of education in public schools, it puts tremendous pressure on schools to ensure that students perform well on standardized tests in math and science. But as a result, physical education and health classes have been minimized—crippled, even—since tests aren't given in those subject areas.

So while some form of nutrition education is offered in many schools, it's very limited because the government doesn't see it as a priority.

"Until more money for federally funded school food programs and a mandate for nutrition education are in place, we'll always be in this situation," says Wilson. "We need a major support from our national government."

Interestingly, there may be a parallel between today's childhood obesity epidemic and the youth smoking problem from the 1970s, says Marlene Schwartz, Ph.D., the director of research and school programs for the Rudd Center for Food Policy and Obesity at Yale University. Back then, Schwartz recalls, no one thought the situation would improve. But as education matched preventive measures, children became informed and behaviors changed.

A 2007 University of Michigan study found that only 22 percent of high-school seniors said they had smoked a cigarette in the previous 30 days, compared to 1976 when the number was 39 percent.

The big changes didn't begin, though, until the mid-1990s, when the government began to make it more difficult for the tobacco industry to target America's youth, according to the report.

Dr. Schumacher has seen the impact of this type of childrens' nutrition education in the research he's conducted. "Recently, one of our children went home for dinner and saw his father pouring ketchup all over his food," recalls Dr. Schumacher. "This fourth-grade kid took the bottle and said, 'Dad, you need to read this label. Look how much sugar you just put on that.' And I thought, Wow."

Children answering health questions rather than asking them? Maybe that's the true solution to the obesity epidemic.

TWELVE

Soft Drink Availability at Schools Has Been Curtailed

Marian Burros

> Marian Burros, a noted cookbook author, is currently writing articles for Rodale.com on First Lady Michelle Obama's initiative to combat childhood obesity in America. *Rodale* is the authoritative source for trusted content in health, fitness, and wellness around the world. In the following viewpoint Burros notes the success of soft drink companies in their compliance with School Beverage Guidelines. Since the 2004–2005 school year, the soft drink industry has driven an 88 percent reduction in total calories from beverages delivered to schools. The decrease is a result of voluntary guidelines adapted by a number of beverage distributors; these guidelines have led to the replacement of many full-calorie beverages with juice and bottled water.

Considering that everyone is talking about the epidemic in childhood obesity—including the first lady, who is working to make the problem disappear in a generation—it may come as some surprise to learn that there has been an 88 percent reduction in calories from not-so-good-for-you beverages like sodas and sports drinks sold in schools across the country since 2004.

Removing Soft Drinks from Schools

But that's just what former President Bill Clinton announced yesterday [March 10, 2010]. His statement comes three years after the Alliance for a Healthier Generation, a joint initiative of the William J. Clinton Foundation and the American Heart Association, teamed with the three top soft drink companies to voluntarily remove sweetened soft drinks from schools across the country, in response to the growing threat of lawsuits and state legislation. Sodas have been replaced by "lower-calorie, nutritious beverage options in age-appropriate portions," according to the American Beverage Association, the trade association for many beverage companies.

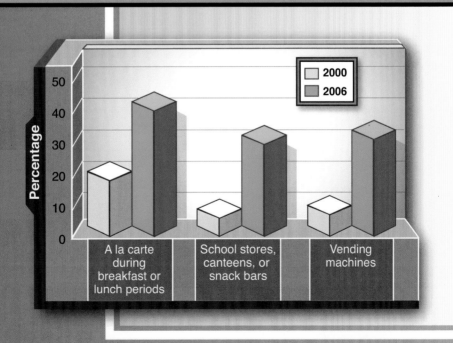

The Percentage of States That Require Schools to Prohibit Offering Junk Foods* in School Settings, 2000 and 2006

* Defined as foods or beverages that have low nutrient density

Taken from: Centers for Disease Control and Prevention. www.cdc.gov.

The details: Shipments of full-calorie soft drinks to schools declined by 95 percent between the first semester of the 2004–2005 school year and the first semester of 2009–2010. Juice drink shipments decreased by 94 percent during that period. In fact, sales of all drinks sold to high schools, which have most of the school beverage vending machines, have dropped dramatically, about 72 percent, in the same period. That includes healthy drinks like water. While bottled water is now the most popular drink sold in schools, it still declined by about 15 percent.

President Clinton was thrilled with the outcome. "Even a person as optimistic as I am, I have to admit I am stunned by the results," he said during a press event focusing on the change.

In May 2006 President Bill Clinton (left), representing his William J. Clinton Foundation, joins Cadbury Schweppes America chief executive officer Gilbert Cassagne to announce an agreement to halt nearly all sales of soda to public schools.

Still Work to Be Done

Health Professionals, however, were a little less enthusiastic. While acknowledging that the beverage association had made "great progress," Margo Wootan, director of nutrition policy at the Center for Science in the Public Interest (CSPI), said, "There is still work to be done." . . .

Read on for tips on choosing healthy beverages.

What it means: Marion Nestle, PhD, MPH [master of public health], Paulette Goddard Professor in the department of nutrition, food studies, and public health at New York University, and author of *What to Eat* (North Point Press, 2006), admits that she finds the news "totally amazing," expressing surprise at the phenomenon of the beverage industry trumpeting a drop in the sales of their products. "The beverage people are spinning loss of sales in every category, even water, as an *improvement?* That's what I'd call it, but I'm not in the soda business," she says. But, like Wootan, she's also concerned that partial success is being taken as total victory. "If nobody is buying this stuff, let's get the vending machines out of schools altogether," Nestle says. "And bring back water fountains. What a concept."

But the beverage industry, says Nestle, is reluctant to give up its foothold in the nation's schools. "They know the next step is getting vending machines out of schools altogether and are doing everything they can to keep those machines there—even to the point of reducing can sizes and using products with less sugar." Among the drinks still permitted under the deal that was brokered are sports drinks, which Nestle describes as "marginally better than regular sodas," and juice drinks, which often have very little fruit juice in them at all.

Snapple is a good example. The main ingredients of its juices are water and concentrates of apple, grape, or pear. When New York City threw soft drinks out of their schools and replaced them with Snapple in 2003, CSPI executive director Michael Jacobson didn't think much of the switch. "They are vitamin-fortified and they don't have caffeine, but they are still pretty much the same as a 12-ounce Coke," he said then. . . .

Limiting Soft Drinks

Don't keep soft drinks in the house. If you want to give your kids a soft drink as a treat, go out and buy it. "That changes things from 'It's normal to drink this all the time' to 'This is something special.'"

Look for 100, avoid concentrates. For parents looking to clear the thicket of 100 percent juice versus juice drinks, there are a couple of guideposts. It's simple enough to look for labels that say "100 percent juice." But if there is a long list of ingredients on the label, it's likely that there is some form of added sugar. It may be masquerading under the name of some kind of fruit juice concentrate—apple, grape, or pear concentrate may sound healthy, but they're heavily processed, and generally stripped of everything but their sweetness. They are much sweeter than simple juice squeezed from an apple or a pear.

Limit it to a glass a day. In any case, nutritionists say children should not drink more than four to 12 ounces of juice daily, depending on age. Even 100 percent juices contain a lot of sugar and calories, without the fiber found in whole fruit (orange and grapefruit juice may be an exception, if they include pulp), and not much else. Keeping overall juice intake low means you spend less time deciphering labels. Give the kids a piece of real fruit instead!

THIRTEEN

Companies Should Be Regulated When Marketing Fast Food to Children

Justin Macmullan

> Justin Macmullan is head of campaigns for Consumers International (CI). Based in the United Kingdom, CI is a federation of consumer groups dedicated to protecting consumers around the world. In this selection Macmullan criticizes the fast food industry for marketing unhealthy products to children. He discusses the organization's belief that the issue of marketing unhealthy food to children is especially important because of the obesity epidemic. In response to aggressive marketing campaigns by fast food companies and the growing obesity problem, CI has offered a number of recommendations focused on regulating unhealthy food. The organization contends that fast food advertising should be limited when aimed at children under the age of sixteen; it also argues for an international code that sets advertising standards when marketing food to children.

Levels of obesity and overweight have reached epidemic proportions. The World Health Organization (WHO) estimates that globally in 2005 1.6 billion adults were overweight and that this will rise to 2.3 billion in 2015. Over the same period, the

Justin Macmullan, *Fried and Tested: An Examination of the Marketing of Fast Food to Children*. London: Consumer International, 2009. Reproduced by permission.

number of obese adults will rise from 400 million to 700 million. Contrary to popular perceptions about obesity and overweight comes the fact that it is not just a concern for high income countries, as some of the highest rates of increase now occur in low and middle income countries where the problem of obesity and overweight can be found side by side with that of under nutrition.

Obesity and Overweight

Obesity and overweight are major contributory factors for non-communicable diseases such as heart disease, type 2 diabetes and some cancers. Unlike communicable diseases, the spread of obesity and overweight is not carried by a virus but by changes in lifestyles and diets. As a result there is now a growing international focus on what can be done to improve people's diets and increase physical exercise. In particular it is hoped that strategies to encourage children to eat healthily and exercise more will reduce future rates of obesity and overweight.

The marketing of 'unhealthy' food to children is particularly important as it targets relatively vulnerable consumers who may not have developed their own ideas on diet and who may also struggle to differentiate between marketing and non-marketing. Children who grow up obese or overweight are more likely to suffer premature death and disability in adulthood.

The Fast Food Industry

Fast food has for several years been a target for public health experts and campaigners who allege that it is having a detrimental impact on the population's health. In response, some companies have changed and adapted some of their practices including reformulating products to reduce levels of fat, sugar and salt, providing more information to consumers and committing to changes in their marketing practices.

The three fast food chains covered by this survey were chosen due to their size and international reach—each of them represents a truly global operation with marketing budgets to match.

- *McDonald's* is the largest fast food chain in the world and [according to the company] 'operates 31,000 local restaurants serving more than 58 million people in 118 countries each day.'
- *Burger King* is the second largest fast food hamburger chain in the world and 'operates more than 11,800 restaurants in all 50 US states and in 74 countries and U.S. territories worldwide.'
- *Kentucky Fried Chicken* (KFC) is owned by Yum brands and is 'the world's most popular chicken restaurant chain. There are over 15,000 KFC outlets in 105 countries and territories around the world.'

The Junk Food Generation Campaign

In 2006 the World Health Assembly (WHA) passed a resolution calling on the WHO to make recommendations on the marketing of food to children. The resolution fitted into a wider WHO strategy on diet, physical activity and health.

This strategy stated that, "Food advertising affects food choices and influences dietary habits. Food and beverage advertisements should not exploit children's inexperience or credulity. Messages that encourage unhealthy dietary practices or physical inactivity should be discouraged, and positive, healthy messages encouraged. Governments should work with consumer groups and the private sector (including advertising) to develop appropriate multi-sectoral approaches to deal with the marketing of food to children, and to deal with such issues as sponsorship, promotion and advertising."

In response to the WHA resolution CI [Consumers International], working with the International Obesity Task Force (IOTF), developed a set of recommendations for an international code on the marketing of food and non-alcoholic beverages to children.

The CI/IOTF recommendations call for an international code on the marketing of food to children to be implemented by national governments and food companies.

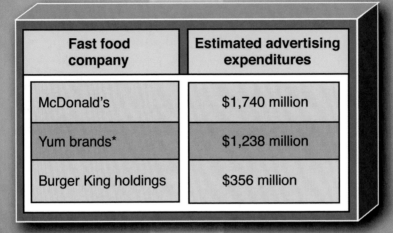

Fast Food Companies' Global Advertising Spending

Fast food company	Estimated advertising expenditures
McDonald's	$1,740 million
Yum brands*	$1,238 million
Burger King holdings	$356 million

* Yum brands is the parent company for Kentucy Fried Chicken, Pizza Hut, Taco Bell, and other fast food outlets.

Taken from: Consumers International, www.consumersinternational.org.

The recommendations target the marketing of energy-dense, nutrient-poor foods that are high in fat, sugar and salt to children up to 16 years old. Its demands include:

- A ban on radio or TV adverts promoting unhealthy food between 06.00 and 21.00 [6:00 A.M. and 9:00 P.M.].
- No marketing of unhealthy food to children using new media (such as websites, social networking sites and text messaging).
- No promotion of unhealthy food in schools.
- No inclusion of free gifts, toys or collectable items, which appeal to children, to promote unhealthy foods.
- No use of celebrities, cartoon characters, competitions or free gifts to market unhealthy food.

In response to campaigning for restrictions on the marketing of food to children the food and drink industry has introduced a number of pledges and commitments. . . .

Slow Changes for Fast Food

Under pressure from health campaigners and consumers, fast food companies appear to have made progress in reformulating their children's menus to reduce the amount of fat, sugar and salt. Whilst some products continue to have high levels of fat or sugar, on the whole the products tended to have low or medium levels of fat, sugar or salt according to the UK FSA [United Kingdom Food Standards Agency] Traffic Light labelling criteria used in this report. Many of the fast food outlets covered by this survey also offered 'healthier' options as part of the children's menu, which gives parents and carers the opportunity to choose items for their children with lower levels of fat, sugar and salt.

However this should not be taken as a sign that fast food is now a healthy option. As this survey has shown, some fast food meals that are marketed to young children can contribute 40% to 60% of a child's GDA [guideline daily amounts] for fat, sugar or salt. And when children outgrow the children's menu and start to choose meals from the adult menu, levels of fat, sugar and salt can increase dramatically. Many of the fast food chains' signature meals were found to contain between 40 and 60% of a 15 to 18 year old boy's GDA for fat and salt, as well as significant levels of saturated fat and sugar, these levels are even higher for girls and for children aged between 11 and 14.

Whilst meals that contain such high levels of fat, sugar and salt may be acceptable when eaten as a main meal or as an occasional treat, for children that visit fast food chains regularly or who are consuming fast food products, or even meals, as a snack between main meals this could contribute towards a problem with over-weight or obesity.

The survey conducted by CI's UK member organisation, Which?, showed that many children in the UK are visiting fast food chains more than once a week and consuming more than

40% of their GDA for fat, sugar and salt during their visit. The use of collectable gifts is just one example of how fast food chains may be encouraging regular visits.

Other studies support the fact that regular visits to fast food chains can be a cause for concern. In particular there have been a number of studies in the US that have shown that a school's proximity to fast food outlets can contribute to an increase in the incidence of overweight in children. For example researchers at Columbia University and the University of California, Berkeley assessed the fitness levels of ninth graders in California schools located near fast food retailers. Obesity rates were significantly higher in those schools a tenth of a mile or less from fast food outlets.

Marketing Meals High in Fat, Sugar, and Salt

Whilst CI welcomes companies' efforts to reformulate products and offer healthier options it is a major concern that all the fast food companies covered by this survey continue to use marketing to promote meals to young children that can constitute such a high proportion of their GDA for fat, sugar and salt.

Whilst the companies are, in some cases, identifying healthier items to parents and carers, they continue to promote meals with relatively high levels of fat, sugar and salt to children. This potentially undermines parents' and carers' efforts to encourage children to eat healthier diets and misses an important opportunity to support healthy eating amongst children.

There is also a concern that marketing burgers, fries and fizzy drinks to young children—even when they are not high in fat, sugar or salt—may be creating a taste for these products in later life. James McNeal, a well-known children's marketing guru and the author of *Kids As Customers*, has said, "We have living proof of the long-lasting quality of early brand loyalties in the cradle-to-grave marketing at McDonald's, and how well it works. We start taking children in for their first and second birthdays, and on and on, and eventually they have a great deal of preference

The McDonald's corporation has used Ronald McDonald to market Happy Meals to children for decades. Critics say that junk food advertising that specifically targets children must end.

for that brand. Children can carry that with them through a lifetime."

As has been noted above, whilst children's fast food meals can contribute a relatively high proportion of a child's GDA, the adult menu contributes even more, with levels of salt and saturated fat particularly high. . . .

Recommendations

CI believes that all children up to the age of 16 years old should be protected from marketing of unhealthy food and drink through a global standard based on the Recommendations prepared by CI and the IOTF.

In particular, the following marketing techniques should not be allowed to promote food high in fat, sugar and/or salt:

1. Advertising or promotion that directly appeals to children, including the:
   - Use of celebrities
   - Use of cartoon characters, including brand owned and licensed
   - Inclusion of free gifts, toys or collectable items
   - Inclusion of competitions, vouchers or games
   - Shape or novelty value of the food or food packaging

2. Advertising or promotion in places children visit frequently, which includes:
   - Nurseries, pre-school centres, schools and school grounds
   - Children's clubs, centres, playgrounds and sports halls
   - Family and child clinics and paediatric services

3. Advertising that targets parents or carers:
   - No indirect advertising to parents or other adults caring for children such as other family members, child carers, teachers, health workers. This includes suggesting that a parent or adult who purchases such a food or beverage for a child is a better, more intelligent or a more generous parent or adult than one who does not do so, or that their child when fed these products will be more intelligent and gifted.

FOURTEEN

The Desire for Junk Food Is Emotional

Geneen Roth

Geneen Roth is an international teacher and the author of books that focus on emotion and food. In this selection Roth discusses the connection between food and relationships within families. She suggests that in some families, parental concern over a child's eating habits is unhealthy. A child who overeats junk food may wish for no more than a parent's attention. Often, Roth states, a parent's concern can be traced to the parent's own childhood. The key to promoting healthier eating habits is to develop a healthier emotional relationship with food.

A mother of an 8-year-old was desperate. "My daughter is gaining weight by the second," she told me. "I am so afraid that I have passed on my troubles with food to her, and I don't know whether to remove all candy from the house, take her to a doctor, or put her on a strict diet. Help!"

"What is your daughter's favorite food?" I asked.

"Chocolate," she said.

"Does high cholesterol, high blood pressure, or diabetes run in your family?"

"No," she said.

"Is your daughter's health good?"

"Yes."

Geneen Roth, "The Junk Food Gene," *Good Housekeeping*, March 2009. Reproduced by permission of the author.

Desperation calls for radical measures, so I said, "On your way home, stop at the store and buy enough chocolate to fill an entire kitchen cabinet. In your kitchen, designate one cabinet The Chocolate Cabinet and fill it to overflowing with the chocolate you bought. Now, tell your daughter that this is hers and hers alone. Tell her that she can eat as much of it as she wants and that you will fill it back up when the cabinet gets even a tiny bit empty. Do not criticize her. Do not watch her with hawk eyes. And make sure that cabinet is brimming with chocolate. Wait three weeks, and then let me know what happens."

She looked at me in disbelief. "Have you lost your mind? If I give Gracie free rein over chocolate, she will devour every single piece before I can get to the store and buy more. She will gain a million pounds. I will create a monster!"

"Try it," I said. "Let's see what happens."

The Chocolate Plan

Fast-forward three weeks. The desperate mother says, "When I first told Gracie about the new plan, she didn't believe me. She waited until I left the kitchen, and then she plowed through the contents of her cabinet before I could change my mind. I filled up that cabinet four times that first week (with gritted teeth, I admit). But when Gracie realized I was not going to criticize her and that I was absolutely serious about letting her have as much as she wanted, she ate less and less. By the second week, I only had to buy a little chocolate, and by the third week, none at all. She is more relaxed around food. She is losing weight. I am a chocolate-cabinet convert!"

Does this story (it's true, by the way) make you excited? Slightly hysterical? Have you come up with 25 reasons why this wouldn't work at your house? You are not alone.

However, while some of your reasons may be based on fact, most of them are about your own relationship to food and hunger and abundance, not your children's. And here's the litmus test:

Some parents have found the chocolate plan, in which kids are allowed to eat as much chocolate as they wish, to be an effective technique in reducing cravings for the treat.

Ask yourself what would happen if you filled one cabinet with food you wanted but believed you're not supposed to have. What would happen if you let yourself eat it without criticizing yourself? I can't swear to this, but I bet you have (at least) 25 reasons why that wouldn't work.

It's not about the food. Although the chocolate-cabinet idea was radical, I was almost positive that what Gracie wanted wasn't candy. She wanted her mother's (positive) attention. She wanted her mother to trust her. But mostly, she wanted to believe in and trust herself, and the only way she could do that was by first learning those skills from her mother. The drama around food and weight gain was the language that Gracie was using to communicate with her mother. The real issue is never the food.

Parental Approval and Food

My mother was a fat kid whose own mother took her shopping in the Chubby section of Macy's. Growing up, my mother felt self-conscious, ashamed of her body around boys, clothes, socializing. Because she loved me and didn't want me to suffer the way she had, when I was a kid she began watching what I ate, restricting certain foods from my diet, telling me I was getting fat.

How did the hawk-eye, restrictive approach work?

Not so well. In response, I began hiding frozen Milky Ways in my pajama pants, sprinting past my parents' room and sitting over the trash can in my room eating the candybars as fast as I could, ready to spit them out if my mother opened the door and caught me. I began feeling as if I needed to look a certain way for her to love me, eat certain foods for her to approve of me. And so I began living (and eating) a double life: When I was in front of her, I'd eat cottage cheese and chicken without skin. When I was out of her sight, I'd stuff myself with everything I wasn't allowed to eat in her presence. Food became the language of our relationship. And although, as my brother often points out, I've made a career from the dysfunction that resulted, I would not recommend this path to anyone.

When I hold my online workshops, mothers from all over the world ask me questions about food and their children. Mothers from Montana and New Jersey, Thailand and Brazil all have the same concerns. They all love their children and don't want to pass on their pain to their daughters (or sons); some of them have children who are already showing signs of starving themselves or stuffing themselves. They all want to know: How do I best love my child when it comes to food? What will help her the most?

A Positive Relationship with Food

I tell them, "Attend to your own relationship with food first." Be honest with yourself about what you actually believe. Do you believe you can't trust your hunger? That if you really let yourself eat what you want, you'd start at one end of your kitchen and chomp your way across the country? Do you believe there is an abundance of what you need, want, love?

After you begin exploring your own relationship with food, be mindful about what you communicate to your children. Deprivation, force, and shame do not ever, under any circumstances, lead to positive change. If you judge your children, if you create a moral standard about body size, if you withhold approval based on what they weigh, nothing good will come of it. They will begin judging their bodies, hiding their food, defining their worth by what they weigh.

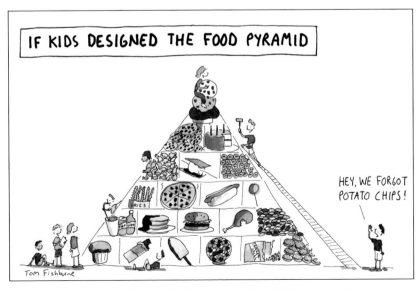

"If Kids Designed the Food Pyramid," illustration by Tom Fishburne, TomFishburne.com. © 2009 Tom Fishburne.

And ask yourself this question: If you could fill a cabinet with anything—food, attention, time—what would it be? Chances are, it won't be chocolate. Commit to being lavish with yourself with what you really need. As you do that, you will become a living example of self-care and trust and love. You will be who you want your children to become. Believe me, they'll notice.

What You Should Know About Junk Food

General Facts About Junk Food

- Every month approximately nine out of ten American children visit a McDonald's restaurant.
- In 1970 Americans spent about $6 billion on fast food. In 2006 the spending rose to nearly $142 billion.
- A supersized order of McDonald's fries contains 610 calories and 29 grams of fat.
- Per ounce, Chicken McNuggets contain twice as much fat as a hamburger.
- There are more than three-hundred thousand fast food restaurants in the United States.
- French fries are the most popular fast food in America. In 1970 french fries surpassed regular potato sales in the United States. In 2004 Americans ate 7.5 billion pounds of frozen french fries.

Junk Food and Obesity

- Less than 25 percent of young people eat the recommended five or more servings of fruits and vegetables each day.
- In America 12.5 million children are overweight, and 13 million more are at serious risk of becoming overweight.
- In 2001 the U.S. surgeon general declared child obesity an epidemic.
- According to the U.S. Department of Agriculture, nine out of ten U.S. schools offer a la carte programs (foods sold outside

the lunch program that do not meet the U.S. government's nutritional recommendations).

- Thirty-four percent of American adults are obese, and 14 percent of children aged two to five are overweight.
- Forty-six percent of Canadian adults are either overweight or obese.
- Studies have shown that a child who is obese between the ages of ten and thirteen has an 80 percent chance of becoming an obese adult.
- Over the last thirty years, the number of overweight children aged six to seventeen has doubled, and more than 25 percent of children aged six to eleven are obese. Among children aged twelve to seventeen, 25 percent of girls and 18 percent of boys are obese.

Junk Food and Advertising

- According to a 2007 Kaiser Family Foundation study, children aged eight to twelve viewed an average of twenty-one food ads per day.
- Of those advertisements, 34 percent were for candy or snacks, 28 percent were for cereal, and 10 percent were for fast food.
- According to the Canadian Pediatric Society, most food advertising on children's television shows is for fast foods, soft drinks, candy, and presweetened cereals.
- A Stanford University study showed that when children aged three to five were offered two identical meals, one wrapped in plain paper and one in McDonald's packaging, children preferred the latter, insisting that it tasted better.
- Over the past twenty-five years, American researchers have found an increase in fast food commercials during children's television programming, with many of these commercials emphasizing larger portions.

Facts About Soft Drinks

- Coca-Cola and PepsiCo products are sold in every country in the world except North Korea.

- During the 1950s the typical soft drink order at a fast food restaurant contained about eight ounces of soda. Today a "child" order of Coke at McDonald's is twelve ounces, and a large Coke is thirty-two ounces (and about 310 calories).
- A can of cola contains ten teaspoons of sugar.
- Fast food companies make higher profits on soft drinks than on food products.
- Twelve- to nineteen-year-old boys drink an average of 868 cans of soda per year; girls drink approximately 651 cans per year.

The Harmful Effects of Junk Food
- The regular consumption of junk food is the leading factor in obesity and excess weight.
- Consumption of soft drinks containing sugar has been linked to weight gain and an increased risk for development of type 2 diabetes.
- Studies have revealed that obese people have twice the rate of chronic health problems as people of normal weight.
- A junk food diet is a major cause of heart disease.

What You Should Do About Junk Food

In recent years a number of controversies have developed around junk food. Researchers have argued that there is a connection between inexpensive junk food and what has been called the obesity epidemic. The medical profession has also argued that junk food—soft drinks, potato chips, and fast food—often take the place of more nutritious food. Social commentators, meanwhile, have been critical of the junk food industry, accusing the industry of advertising directly to children and teenagers and of selling products in schools. Finally, a number of politicians have begun to consider the possibility of taxing junk food, arguing that the tax money can be used to pay for health care costs.

Despite the level of criticism, many remain unconvinced that junk food is harmful. Stanley Feldman goes so far as to insist that there is no such thing as junk food because even a fast food hamburger has certain nutritional value. The problem with junk food, he and others argue, is that people simply consume too much of it. Others argue that the connection between junk food and obesity is difficult to prove; theoretically, a person could eat junk food but remain slender because of exercise. Finally, many people have argued that a tax on junk food is simply an excuse for governments to raise more money and will not change how much people are consuming.

Learn More About the Issue

In order to form an opinion and take action on the issues surrounding junk food, it is important to know more about the current debate. You might begin by gathering magazine articles and Internet information about junk food. Who decides what foods qualify as junk food? How long have people referred to certain kinds of food as "junk" or "fast"? How do those foods differ from nonjunk foods? At what point, in countries like the United States and Britain, did junk food become controversial? At what point did issues around junk food become an international issue? It may also be helpful to research primary documents. Many companies and restaurants that manufacture junk and fast food have publications and Web sites. What information do these companies provide about the nutritional value of their products?

Much of this information can be found in school and public libraries. Whereas encyclopedias and dictionaries are frequently good sources of basic information, more narrowly focused books will address specific issues focusing on junk food. Periodicals and newspapers offer a more immediate, or "ground-level," view of how people have reacted to issues around junk food. Teachers and librarians can also suggest how to access resources specific to your school, including the nutritional values of the school lunch program and the school's policy on vending machines.

Define the Debate

As with any contentious issue, there are many sides to the debate that has formed around junk food. Understanding these various positions will help define the parameters of that debate. Organizations representing different viewpoints frequently have pamphlets and other materials outlining their positions. Most organizations also have Internet sites, allowing easy access to an organization's current activities and even providing links to like-minded sites.

As you gather information from various sites, what are the recurring ideas within the broader issues that form around junk food? Do certain organizations focus on a limited set of ideas within the debate or approach the issues around junk food more generally? Are the ideas that each organization focuses on related to contemporary controversies, or do these ideas relate to long-running questions within the junk food debate? Other information, such as surveys from various polling organizations, can help clarify how the broader public views the issues surrounding junk food.

Finally, you can learn more about the issue by attending a meeting of the local school board that addresses an issue surrounding junk food, such as vending machines on school property. What are the opinions of the teachers, parents, and students involved? How are these arguments similar to or different from the arguments presented by organizations that address junk food issues?

Form an Opinion

Ultimately, learning more about and defining the debate around junk food offers the groundwork needed to begin forming your own opinion. As you read various viewpoints about junk food, perhaps you agreed with some, disagreed with others, and remained undecided about others. It is possible that you will find an organization whose views you share, but it is just as likely that you will find plausible points in multiple organizations. As you weigh the various arguments, you might also question how your opinions have been formed. Are they the same as your parents' or guardians' or teachers'? Have they changed on specific junk food issues over time or remained the same? Have your opinions been formed by secondary observation or actual experience?

Many arguments—both pro and con—may also seem abstract unless you have lived through them. One method of forming an opinion would be to ask yourself how you would think or feel in a particular situation. For instance, how would you feel if your school removed all vending machines? Would you feel that your rights had been violated? Or would you agree that schools have the right to make decisions that may impact student health?

You might also consider an example from your own experience. For instance, consider how much fast and junk food your friends and family eat each day. Do these junk food items replace other, perhaps healthier food choices? Do you believe that there is a relationship between junk and fast food and being overweight?

Take Action

Forming an opinion on the issues surrounding junk food may also inspire you to take action. This might include writing a letter to the editor of the local newspaper about a junk food tax or perhaps writing a letter to your school board about a vending machine policy. Many people get involved with issues by joining an organization, and many organizations sponsor activities ranging from contacting government officials to staging public rallies. Other possibilities include forming your own organization with like-minded friends and starting a blog on the Internet.

Despite whether you decide to take action on the issues surrounding junk food, your research and background information will help you to make informed decisions about the debate. You will not only understand the history and parameters of the junk food argument, but you will also be capable of adding valuable input and explaining your own position on the issue.

ORGANIZATIONS TO CONTACT

American Diabetes Association (ADA)
1701 N. Beauregard St., Alexandria, VA 22311
(800) 342-2383
e-mail: askada@diabetes.org
Web site: www.diabetes.org

The ADA, a not-for-profit health advocacy organization, works to prevent and cure diabetes. As a part of its program, the association provides a guide to eating out and tips for how to order healthier items while dining at restaurants and fast food establishments.

American Obesity Association
8630 Fenton St., Ste. 814, Silver Spring, MD 20910
(301) 563-6526
Web site: www.obesity.org

The American Obesity Association is the leading scientific organization dedicated to the study of obesity and its health effects. Its researchers seek to understand the causes and treatment of obesity while also keeping the medical community informed of the latest advances in research. It publishes the journal *Obesity*, and several newsletters and reports found on its Web site discuss the effects of fast food on obesity.

Center for Science in the Public Interest (CSPI)
1875 Connecticut Ave. NW, Ste. 300,
Washington, DC 20009-5728
(202) 332-9110
e-mail: cspi@cspinet.org
Web site: www.cspinet.org

Formed in 1971, the CSPI is a nonprofit education and consumer advocacy organization dedicated to fighting for government food policies and corporate practices that promote healthy diets. The center also works to prevent deceptive marketing practices and ensures that science is used for public welfare. It publishes the *Nutrition Action Healthletter,* the most widely circulated health newsletter in North America.

Centers for Disease Control and Prevention (CDC)
Division of Nutrition and Physical Activity (DNPA)
1600 Clifton Rd., Atlanta, GA 30333
(800) 232-4636
e-mail: cdcinfo@cdc.gov
Web site: www.cdc.gov/nccdphp/dnpa

The CDC is part of the Department of Health and Human Services. Its Division of Nutrition and Physical Activity (DNPA) has three focus areas: nutrition, physical activity, and obesity. The DNPA addresses the role of nutrition and physical activity in improving the public's health. DNPA activities include health promotion, research, training, and education. The DNPA maintains an archive of articles on its Web site, many of which are about the relationship between obesity and fast food.

Food and Drug Administration (FDA)
10903 New Hampshire Ave., Silver Spring, MD 20993
(888) 463-6332
Web site: www.fda.gov

The FDA is the public health agency charged with protecting American consumers by enforcing the Federal Food, Drug, and Cosmetic Act and several related public health laws. The agency sends investigators and inspectors into the field to ensure that the country's almost ninety-five thousand FDA-regulated businesses are compliant. Its publications include government documents, reports, fact sheets, and press announcements. It also provides food labeling guidance and regulatory information for restaurants on its Web site.

Food Marketing Institute
2345 Crystal Dr., Ste. 800, Arlington, VA 22202
(202) 452-8444 • fax: (202) 429-4519
Web site: www.fmi.org

The Food Marketing Institute conducts programs in public affairs, food safety, research and education, and industry relations on behalf of food retailers and wholesalers in the United States and around the globe. The "Health and Wellness" section on its Web site provides information about nutrition, nutrition labeling, and obesity.

Food Research and Action Center (FRAC)
1875 Connecticut Ave. NW, Ste. 540, Washington, DC 20009
(202) 986-2200
Web site: www.frac.org

FRAC is the leading national nonprofit organization working to improve public policies and public and private partnerships to eradicate hunger and malnutrition in the United States. The center serves as a watchdog of regulations and policies affecting the poor. It conducts public information campaigns, including the Campaign to End Childhood Hunger, to ensure that children of low-income families receive healthy and nutritious food so that they are able to learn and grow.

Healthy Refrigerator
1100 Johnson Ferry Rd., Ste. 300, Atlanta, GA 30319
(404) 252-3663.
Web site: www.healthyfridge.org

The Healthy Refrigerator includes nutrition and health recommendations for children and adults along with recipes, articles, and quizzes. A "Just for Kids" section offers facts about heart disease and a "healthy fridge" quiz.

National Council of Chain Restaurants (NCCR)
325 Seventh St. NW, Ste. 1100, Washington, DC 20004
(800) 673-4692
e-mail: grannisk@nrf.com
Web site: www.nccr.net

The NCCR is the national trade association representing the chain restaurant industry and its 125,000 facilities. The council works to advance sound public policy that best serves the interests of chain restaurants and the 3 million people they employ. Its Web site provides up-to-date industry news, links to a number of government-relations resources, and a legislative action center where viewers can research legislation and learn how to work with Congress. Members of the site have access to the *NCCR Highlights Newsletter*.

National Restaurant Association
1200 Seventeenth St. NW, Washington, DC 20036
(202) 331-5900
e-mail: webchef@restaurant.org
Web site: www.restaurant.org

The National Restaurant Association represents, educates, and promotes America's $566 billion restaurant business. It promotes a pro-restaurant agenda, argues on behalf of the restaurant industry before Congress and federal regulatory agencies, and works to battle antirestaurant initiatives. Reports, publications, press releases, and research about important topics affecting the food industry can all be found on its Web site, including the *2009 Restaurant Industry Forecast*.

U.S. Department of Agriculture (USDA)
Food and Nutrition Service
1400 Independence Ave. SW, Washington, DC 20250
(202) 720-2791
Web site: www.usda.gov

The Food and Nutrition Service, an agency of the USDA, is responsible for administering the nation's domestic nutrition assistance programs. It provides prepared meals, food assistance, and nutrition education materials to one in five Americans. The agency also encourages children and teens to follow the healthy eating guidelines set by MyPyramid in its Eat Smart, Play Hard campaign.

BIBLIOGRAPHY

Books

Hank Cardello and Doug Garr, *Stuffed: An Insider's Look at Who's (Really) Making America Fat*. New York: Ecco, 2009.

Greg Crister, *Fat Land: How Americans Became the Fattest People in the World*. New York: Mariner, 2004.

Nancy Deville, *Death by Supermarket: The Fattening, Dumbing Down, and Poisoning of America*. Fort Lee, NJ: Barricade, 2007.

Eric A. Finklestein, *The Fattening of America: How the Economy Makes Us Fat, If It Matters, and What to Do About It*. Hoboken, NJ: Wiley, 2008.

John A. Jakle and Keith A. Sculle, *Fast Food: Roadside Restaurants in the Automobile Age*. Baltimore: Johns Hopkins University Press, 1999.

Joseph Mercola and Ben Lerner, *Generation XL: Raising Healthy, Intelligent Kids in a High-Tech, Junk-Food World*. Nashville: Thomas Nelson, 2007.

Marion Nestle, *Food Politics: How the Food Industry Influences Nutrition and Health*. Berkeley and Los Angeles: University of California Press, 2002.

———, *What to Eat*. New York: North Point, 2006.

Michael Pollan, *In Defense of Food: An Eater's Manifesto*. New York: Penguin, 2009.

Eric Schlosser, *Fast Food Nation*. New York: HarperPerennial, 2000.

Michele Simon, *Appetite for Profit: How the Food Industry Undermines Our Health and How to Fight Back*. New York: Nation, 2006.

Brian Wansink, *Mindless Eating: Why We Eat More than We Think*. New York: Bantam, 2007.

Karl Weber, ed., *Food Inc.: A Participant Guide; How Industrial Food Is Making Us Sicker, Fatter, and Poorer, and What You Can Do About It*. Philadelphia: Public Affairs, 2009.

Charles Wilson and Eric Schlosser, *Chew on This: Everything You Don't Want to Know About Fast Food*. New York: Sandpiper, 2007.

Periodicals and Internet Sources

Catherine Arnst, "A Tobacco-Style Tax on Fattening Drinks," *Business Week Online*, January 12, 2009. www.businessweek.com.

————, "Taxing the Rich—Foods, That Is," *Business Week Online*, February 23, 2009. www.businessweek.com.

Catherine Brahic, "Marine Animals Go Hungry on Junk Food Diet," *New Scientist*, June 21, 2008.

Linda Buchwald, "Learning from Labels," *Scholastic Choices*, November/December 2009.

Claire Connors, "The Health That Got Me Fit," *Shape*, February 2009.

Thale Dillon, "Too Much Junk Food and TV 'Obesity Epidemic' on Upward Trajectory," *Montana Business Quarterly*, Winter 2009.

George Dohrmann, "I Want My Body Back," *Sports Illustrated*, June 8, 2009.

Meagan Francis, "Healthy Eats for Kids," *Natural Health*, September 2009.

Bob Garfield, "Junk-Food Ads That Promote 'Random Acts' Are Irresponsible," *Advertising Age*, May 26, 2008.

Emma Hall, "In Europe, the Clash over Junk-Food Heats Up," *Advertising Age*, March 5, 2007.

Stephanie Liberatore, "Health Wise," *Science Teacher*, September 2008.

Karen Linamen, "Put the Candy Down! How to Stop Mindless Eating and Other Naughty Habits," *Today's Christian Woman*, January/February 2009.

Jennifer Magid, "Just Junk? See What's Really in Your Favorite Fun Foods," *Current Health 2*, February 2010.

Alice Oglethorpe, "'I Finally Got It Right,'" *Shape*, February 2009.

Celeste Perrino-Walker, "Eat What I Say (and Not What I Eat)," *Vibrant Life*, March/April 2009.

Anna Lena Phillips, "Junk Food: It Really Can Kill You—If You're a Condor Chick," *American Scientist*, September/October 2007.

Laurie K. Schenden, "It's Feeding Time," *Curve*, November 2008.

Gordon M. Verber, "Diabetes, Junk Food, and Sleep," *Science News*, March 14, 2009.

Adam Voiland, "No License to Overindulge," *U.S. News & World Report*, June 18, 2007.

INDEX

impact of soft drinks on,
66–71

Healthy food
is more expensive for school
districts, 84–85
tax on fast food would allow
subsidization of, 49–50

Healthy foods, fat content of,
junk food *vs.*, *19*

Heart disease, 52, 74
soft drink consumption and,
69–70

I

International Obesity Task
Force (IOTF), 95–96

Ismail, Amid, 69

Ivester, M. Douglas, 66–67

J

Jacobson, Michael F., 62

Journal of Public Economics, 55

Journal of Public Health, 10

*Journal of the American Medical
Association*, 10

Juice
calories per serving in, *vs.*
soft drinks, *76*
choosing healthy forms of,
92
soft drinks are no more
unhealthy than, 72–78

Juice Producers Association,
75

Junk food
desire for, is emotional,
101–106

fat content of, healthy foods
vs., *19*
food industry tries to alter
perceptions of, 9–14
government should not
regulate, 56–61
impacts on agriculture,
35–36
as international issue, 5, 8
is as addictive as drugs,
30–39
is not as addictive as drugs,
40–45
percent of Americans
choosing, when under
stress, *34*
percentage of states
prohibiting schools from
offering, 89
in schools, National School
Lunch Program (NSLP)
contributes to, 79–87
should be taxed, 46–50
tax on
in Romania, 6–7
will not decrease junk food
consumption, 51–55
there is no such thing as,
15–23

Junk food companies, do not
offer healthy alternatives,
24–29

K

Kaplan, Karen, 72

Keller, Thomas, 30

Kentucky Fried Chicken
  (KFC), 36
  size of, 95
Kessler, David, 37, 38, 40
Kidney stones, cola drink
  consumption and, 70–71
Kids As Customers (McNeal),
  98

L
Ludwig, David, 10
Lustig, Robert, 75, 78

M
Macmullan, Justin, 93
Mayo Clinic, 68
McDonald's, 15, 16, 36–37,
  38–39, 99
  expansion in Romania, 5
  global advertising spending
    by, 96
  McGriddle product of, 38–39
  size of, 95
McMichael, Philip, 35
McNeal, James, 98
Meat
  processed, as predigested,
    37–38
  reclaimed, 22–23
Michael, Paul, 46

N
National Health and
  Nutrition Examination
  Survey, 63
National Institute of Diabetes
  and Digestive and Kidney
  Diseases (NIDDK), 70

National Longitudinal Study
  of Adolescent Health, 55
National Osteoporosis
  Foundation, 67
National School Lunch
  Program, is flawed and
  contributes to junk food in
  schools, 79–87
National Soft Drink
  Association, 66
Nestlé, 5
Nestle, Marion, 10, 11, 13,
  24, 91
*Neuroscience Biobehavior
  Review* (journal), 41
New York Times (newspaper),
  32, 35
No Child Left Behind Act
  (2001), 86–87
Nutritional guidelines, are
  made confusing due to food
  industry pressure, 13–14

O
Obama, Michelle, 8
Obesity/overweight
  adult, prevalence in U.S., 47
  in children, school programs
    to combat, 86
  global prevalence of, 93–94
  health effects of, 52, 67, 94
  juice consumption and,
    75–76
  prevalence among children
    in U.S., 9–10
  in Romania, 5–6
  soft drink consumption and,
    67